TRANSACTIONS

of the

American Philosophical Society

Held at Philadelphia for Promoting Useful Knowledge

VOLUME 79, Part 5

The Virtuous Pagan

In Middle English Literature

Cindy L. Vitto

THE AMERICAN PHILOSOPHICAL SOCIETY

Independence Square, Philadelphia

1989

Library of Congress Catalog
Card Number 89-84934
International Standard Book Number 0–87169–795–5
US ISSN 0065–9746

TABLE OF CONTENTS

I. INTRODUCTION

For pious Christians of every age, the question of ultimate concern has been salvation: What is necessary to ensure the soul's eternal bliss? During the Middle Ages, this issue became increasingly complex. Within the Church itself, the guidelines were quite clear: baptism, reception of the sacraments, an attempt to put into practice the teachings of Christ. But a theological debate arose on a corollary issue, the possibility of salvation for those outside the Church.[1] These non-Christians fell into two basic categories: those who had been offered the Christian faith but had refused it, and those who, for reasons of chronology or geography, lacked the opportunity to join the Church but lived as virtuously as possible in light of their circumstances. Two categories of these "virtuous pagans" who received special attention were the classical poets and philosophers of Greece and Rome, and the Old Testament patriarchs. From the standpoint of human reason, it seemed especially unfortunate—even unfair, were one presumptuous enough to question God's judgment—that these two groups should be damned eternally.

From the first through the fourteenth centuries, a succession of solutions to the problem of these virtuous pagans evolved. For the early Church, an attractive solution was that Christ descended into Hell to convert the souls He found there. After Augustine refuted this idea, in the early Middle Ages there developed in some detail the idea of Limbo as an intermediate state between bliss and punishment. Aquinas sanctioned the concept of Limbo, and Dante expanded and schematized an elaborate cosmological framework in which most of the classical pagans resided. Aquinas had also, however, given the impetus to the fourteenth century's emphasis on the salvation of pagans during their lifetime. If a man ignorant of Christianity followed the natural virtues as closely as possible, God could lead him to the faith necessary for his soul's salvation. More extreme theologians advanced the view that God exercised the power to choose those He wished to save, regardless of their beliefs or actions.

---

[1] Cyprian's famous maxim "Salus extra Ecclesiam non est," often misquoted as "Nulla salus extra Ecclesiam," became a Christian commonplace. Yet its stern finality is balanced by another commonplace, this one from Erasmus: "Sancte Socrates, ora pro nobis." From the era of the early Church, through the Middle Ages, and beyond, Christian thinkers have ranged themselves on one side or the other on the issue of heathen salvation, even managing to find compromises so that the two views are not necessarily contradictory. An incisive overview of the problem is offered by Craig R. Thompson in his commentary (pp. 100–121) in *Erasmus: Inquisitio de Fide,* 2nd ed. (1950; Hamden, Conn.: Archon Books, 1975).

1

Complicating this matter was the question of the prerequisites for salvation. Theologians tended to divide between those who valued the role of reason in attaining faith (thus making salvation a distinct possibility for pagans, especially the classical philosophers) and those who emphasized faith alone (thus effectively closing the door to non-Christians). An ancillary problem developed in relation to the necessity for baptism, and on what constituted baptism.

Although the issue of the virtuous pagan generated disagreement from its first appearance in the early Church, by the fourteenth century a full-scale debate was underway; speculation about the fate of the virtuous pagan appeared in secular as well as theological writings. These secular works reflected varying theological solutions of the problem but generally agreed that the virtuous pagan could indeed be saved—if the pagan's extraordinary righteousness justified his becoming a part of God's plan. This was a conservative view compared to the extremes to which many theologians had carried the issue.

As we shall see, the two authors who are the focus of this study used the issue of the virtuous pagan to relay an important message to their Christian audience. Both are concerned with the relative importance of divine grace and human deeds in attaining salvation, and both are aware of the responsibility of the Church to strengthen believers and convert non-believers. In *St. Erkenwald*, the poet tells the story of a virtuous pagan whose soul was deliberately left behind during Christ's Harrowing of Hell. When Erkenwald, acting as Christ's surrogate, "harrows" this soul through a miraculous baptism, the onlookers are strengthened in their appreciation of grace (made possible by Christ's victory in Hell) as the agent of salvation. At the same time, the miracle of the poem becomes a figurative imperative for the fourteenth-century Church to continue, in a more conventional way, the work of "harrowing" Hell by offering baptism and faith to unbelievers.

Similar concerns appear in *Piers Plowman.* In the *Dowel* section, Langland's dreamer seeks to understand (among other things) the place of baptism and knowledge of doctrine in salvation, important factors in determining the fate of virtuous pagans. At the same time, the poem utilizes the episode of the Harrowing as its thematic climax, for this event determines the distinguishing characteristics of the Old Testament frame in the *Visio*, the New Covenant in *Dobet*, and the impending apocalypse in *Dobest*. In addition, the Harrowing stands as a type of a second Harrowing, the Judgment, which gives urgency to the dreamer's quest and to the situation of the Church Militant.

At this point, few studies have been published which examine in depth the interplay of the theological and literary treatment of the virtuous pagan in fourteenth-century England. Several works have dealt with the overall question of pagan salvation, tracing its development historically and theologically; for example, R.V. Turner's article *"Descendit ad inferos:* Medieval Views on Christ's Descent Into Hell and the Salvation of the

Ancient Just"; Louis Capéran's *Le problème du salut des infidèles;* Mario Frezza's *Il problema della salvezza dei pagina (da Abelardo al Seicento);* and Paul Vignaux's *Justification et prédestination au XIVe siècle.*[2] J. A. MacCulloch's *The Harrowing of Hell,* J. Monnier's *La descente aux enfers: étude de pensée religieuse, d'art et de littérature,* and Gaston Paris' *La légende de Trajan* are more specialized but related studies.[3] In addition, the question of the virtuous pagan as it played a role in the medieval debate between grace and works, God's will and man's, has been examined by Gordon Leff and Janet Coleman, as well as by historians of the fourteenth-century Church.[4] Almost all other works are limited to a consideration of a single author's treatment of the issue of the virtuous pagan.[5]

Only three studies examine the use of prominent theological concerns by the most important secular authors of the fourteenth century. Two of these are unpublished dissertations: John F. McNamara's "Responses to Ockhamist Theology in the Poetry of the *Pearl*-Poet, Langland, and Chaucer," and Thomas Hahn's "God's Friends: Virtuous Heathens in Later Medieval Thought and English Literature."[6] Both works deal with a broad

[2] R. V. Turner, *"Descendit ad inferos:* Medieval Views on Christ's Descent Into Hell and the Salvation of the Ancient Just," *Journal of the History of Ideas* 27 (1966): 173–194. Note also Constance I. Smith's "Reply to *'Descendit ad inferos:* Medieval Views on Christ's Descent Into Hell and the Salvation of the Ancient Just,'" *Journal of the History of Ideas* 30 (1969): 249–250.

Louis Capéran, *Le problème du salut des infidèles* (Toulouse: Grand Séminaire, 1934).

Mario Frezza, *Il problema della salvezza dei pagina (da Abelardo al Seicento)* (Napoli: Fiorentino, 1962).

Paul Vignaux, *Justification et prédestination au XIVe siècle* (Paris: E. Leroux, 1934).

[3] J. A. MacCulloch, *The Harrowing of Hell: A Comparative Study of an Early Christian Doctrine* (Edinburgh: T. and T. Clark, 1930).

J. Monnier, *La descente aux enfers: étude de pensée religieuse, d'art et de littérature* (Paris: Librairie Fischbacher, 1905).

Gaston Paris, *La légende de Trajan* (Paris: Imprimerie Nationale, 1878).

[4] Gordon Leff, *Bradwardine and the Pelagians* (Cambridge: Cambridge University Press, 1957); Janet Coleman, *"Sublimes et Litterati:* The Audience for the Themes of Grace, Justification and Predestination, Traced from the Disputes of the Fourteenth Century *Moderni* to the Vernacular *Piers Plowman,"* Ph.D. diss., Yale University 1970. (See also Coleman's recently published book, *Piers Plowman and the Moderni* [Rome: Edizioni di storia e letteratura, 1981].) Two especially helpful books for general background of the fourteenth-century Church are William Pantin's *The English Church in the Fourteenth Century* (Cambridge: Cambridge University Press, 1955) and J. A. Robson's *Wyclif and the Oxford Schools* (Cambridge: Cambridge University Press, 1961).

[5] For a study of the issue of pagan salvation in Dante, see the following: Gino Rizzo, "Dante and the Virtuous Pagans," in *A Dante Symposium. In Commemoration of the 700th Anniversary of the Poet's Birth (1265–1965),* ed. William DeSua and Gino Rizzo, University of North Carolina Studies in the Romance Languages and Literatures 58 (Chapel Hill, N.C.: University of North Carolina Press, 1965) 115–140; F. Ruffini, "Dante e il problema della salvezza degl'infideli," *Studi danteschi* 14 (1930): 79–92.

The following deal with the theme of the virtuous pagan in *Piers Plowman:* R. W. Chambers, "Long Will, Dante, and the Righteous Heathen," *Essays and Studies by Members of the English Association* 9 (1924): 50–69; Greta Hort, *Piers Plowman and Contemporary Religious Thought* (New York: MacMillan, 1937); T. P. Dunning, "Langland and the Salvation of the Heathen," *Medium Aevum* 12 (1943): 45–54; G. H. Russell, "The Salvation of the Heathen: The Exploration of a Theme in *Piers Plowman,"* *Journal of the Warburg and Courtauld Institute* 29 (1966): 101–116; Denise N. Baker, "From Plowing to Penitence: *Piers Plowman* and Fourteenth Century Theology," *Speculum* 55 (1980): 715–725.

[6] John F. McNamara, "Responses to Ockhamist Theology in the Poetry of the *Pearl*-Poet,

range of literature. McNamara discusses all the works of the *Pearl*-poet
(to whom he also ascribes *St. Erkenwald*), Chaucer's *Troilus and Criseyde,* and
several of the *Canterbury Tales.* Hahn discusses *Mandeville's Travels, Alexander
B, Patience, The Awyntyrs of Arthure, St. Erkenwald, Piers Plowman,* and *Troilus
and Criseyde.* This range of material forces both authors to a certain su-
perficiality in dealing with the literature.

The third study which examines the interplay of fourteenth-century
theology and literature is Gordon Whatley's article "The Uses of Hagiography: The Legend of Pope Gregory and the Emperor Trajan in the
Middle Ages."[7] Whatley does an admirable job of tracing this legend,
central to the virtuous pagan issue, from its earliest appearance in the
eighth century through the fourteenth century. Emphasizing the different
treatments of the legend as it progressed through the centuries, Whatley
demonstrates that Dante, Langland, and Wyclif use the legend as a means
of expressing their dissatisfaction with the fourteenth-century Church
and its representatives. In a related article, "Heathens and Saints: *St.
Erkenwald* in Its Legendary Context," he illustrates that the *Erkenwald*-poet
adopts the opposite stance, providing a "conservative corrective to the
secularist versions of the Gregory/Trajan legend."[8]

The present work differs from these earlier studies in two respects: (1)
It is restricted to a limited body of literature in an effort to explore in
depth the use of the theme of the virtuous pagan; (2) Although the
theological background (lengthy as it must be) provides an indispensable
backdrop, the main emphasis falls on a clearer comprehension of the
literature itself rather than on an evaluation of the theological beliefs of
the authors. It is my hope that a thorough analysis of the issue of the
virtuous pagan will yield rewarding insights as we study *St. Erkenwald* and
Piers Plowman.

Langland, and Chaucer," Ph.D. diss., Louisiana State University 1968; Thomas Hahn, "God's
Friends: Virtuous Heathen in Later Medieval Thought and English Literature," Ph.D. diss.,
UCLA 1974.

   [7] Gordon Whatley, "The Uses of Hagiography: The Legend of Pope Gregory and the
Emperor Trajan in the Middle Ages," *Viator* 15 (1984): 25–63.

   [8] Gordon Whatley, "Heathens and Saints: *St. Erkenwald* in Its Legendary Context," *Speculum*
61 (1986): 330–363; quote from p. 345.

II. THEOLOGICAL BACKGROUND

The Early Church

The issue of the virtuous pagan is frequently linked with the event of Christ's descent into Hell during the three days between His burial and resurrection. This results from the fact that, strictly speaking, all men were pagans before the Christian era commenced with the Incarnation. Accordingly, it was commonly believed that until the Incarnation *all* souls descended into Hell at death. This belief can be traced to the Judaic concept of Sheol, an immense pit under the earth, where all dead were re-united in an elementary form of existence as recognizable shades of themselves.[1] The idea that all the dead of the Old Testament were confined to Hell is confirmed by the words of such men as Jacob ("Descendam ad inferos lugens filium meum" and "Deducetis canos meos cum dolore ad inferos" [Genesis 37:35 and 42:38]), Job ("infernus domus mea est, et in tenebris stravi lectulum meum" [Job 17:13]), David ("Deus redimet animam meam de manu inferi, cum acceperit me" [Psalms 48:16]), and Hezekiah ("Ego dixi: In dimidio dierum meorum vadam ad portas inferi" [Isaiah 38:10]).[2]

There was New Testament support for this idea as well. Chapter 11 of Hebrews, after listing several Old Testament characters who pleased God through their faith, concludes by saying that they did not receive "the promise" but awaited something better (Christ): "et hii omnes testimonio fidei probati non acceperunt repromissionem / Deo pro nobis melius aliquid providente ut ne sine nobis consummarentur" (Hebrews 11:39–40).[3] Thus, with few exceptions, all those who had lived—from Adam up to Christ's lifetime—were housed in Hell.[4] This made Christ's descent into Hell very important, for the effect of His actions on these non-Christians provided a clue to the fate of those pagans who would live and die after the Incarnation. In addition, Christ's actions in Hell might

---

[1] J. Monnier, *La descente aux enfers: étude de pensée religieuse, d'art et de littérature* (Paris: Librairie Fischbacher, 1905) 7. J. A. MacCulloch, in *The Harrowing of Hell: A Comparative Study of an Early Christian Doctrine* (Edinburgh: T. and T. Clark, 1930) 312, contends that the parable of Dives and Lazarus in Luke 16:19–31 probably represents a belief in two divisions of Sheol, one for the righteous and one for the wicked.

[2] I have presented a few of the Old Testament passages which Alain of Lille refers to while presenting this argument in his work *De Fide Catholica: Contra Haereticos, Valdenses, Iudaeos et Paganos.* See *Patrologia Latina* (hereafter referred to as *P.L.*), Vol. 210, cap. xix, col. 418.

[3] *Biblia Sacra Vulgata,* ed. Robertus Weber (Stuttgart: Württembergische Bibelanstalt, 1969).

[4] The exceptions—Enoch, Elijah, and a few others—are discussed on p. 8 below.

help Christians determine the criteria necessary for their own salvation. Accordingly, two questions arose which the early Church attempted to answer: (1) Did Christ actually descend into Hell? (2) What was the purpose of His descent? The Bible, the Apocrypha, and the first- and second-century Fathers generally agreed that Christ had indeed descended into Hell, but several possibilities were advanced as to His purpose there. Also, although it was generally understood that Christ had liberated souls from Hell, the Fathers disagreed about which souls He freed.

On the first matter, the actual occurrence of the Descent, various passages in the Old and New Testaments support the idea. The text which appears to have been cited most often, however, is Hosea 13:14: "I will ransom them from the power of the grave; I will redeem them from death: O death, I will be thy plagues; O grave, I will be thy destruction."[5]

The Descent figures even more prominently in Apocryphal literature. Here, besides an affirmation of the event, we find three major interpretations of Christ's purpose in Hell: to preach to the souls He found there, to battle the devil and establish divine sovereignty, or to baptize those in Hell.

The Apocryphon of Jeremiah, which supports the theory that Christ descended to preach, is quoted by the Church Fathers Justin and Irenaeus: "The Lord God remembered His dead, the saints of Israel that have fallen asleep in the tomb, and He went down unto them, to proclaim the good news of the salvation He was bringing to them."[6] Although this passage indicates that Christ preached only to those who had anticipated His coming, we shall see that Clement and Origen later expanded this concept in the belief that Christ preached to all the souls in Hell.[7]

The Testaments of the Twelve Patriarchs, on the other hand, emphasize Christ's conflict with the devil and the subsequent deliverance of Hell's captives. This aspect is also prominent in the Testament of Levi (IV, 1): "The rocks are rent, and the sun quenched, and the waters dried up. . . . the invisible spirits mourn, and Hell is despoiled through the Passion of the Most High."[8] The Gospel of Nicodemus, perhaps the most detailed account of the Descent, vividly presents the dramatic battle between Christ and Satan.[9] The theatrical appeal of the Descent's cosmic battle

---

[5] The Vulgate version reads, "De manu mortis liberabo eos, de mortes redimam eos; ero mors tua, o mors, morsus tuus ero, inferne." For other Biblical references that have been interpreted as referring to the Descent, see Psalms 23:7–9, Zechariah 9:11, Matthew 12:39–40 and 27:52–53; Acts 2:29 and 2:27–31; Romans 10:7, Ephesians 4:9–10, Colossians 2:15; I Peter 3:18–20 and 4:6.

[6] See Justin, *Dial.* LXXII, 4; and Irenaeus, *Adv. haer.* III, 20:4; IV, 22:1, 33:1, 33:12; V, 31:1. From Jean Daniélou, *The Theology of Jewish Christianity*, trans. John A. Baker (Chicago: H. Regnery Co., 1964) 235.

[7] See pp. 10–11 below.

[8] Daniélou 239–240.

[9] Although this gospel was actually composed in the early fifth century, it is evidently a compilation of older material. See Johannes Quasten, *The Beginnings of Patristic Literature,* Vol. I of *Patrology* (Westminster, Md.: Newman Press, 1951) 116.

was not overlooked by the medieval mystery playwrights; the Harrowing of Hell was granted a separate scene in each of the four English cycles.[10] The scene deserves closer examination, for it introduces two other aspects of the Descent—the idea of Adam as the first freed from Hell and the concept of Christ's deceiving the devil.

In the Gospel of Nicodemus, Satan and Hell are two separate characters who discuss the imminent reception of the Man dying on the cross. Satan rejoices in the defeat of an enemy who has cheated him by healing many and even stealing some of the dead, but Hell is wiser and fears Jesus' power. When a voice rings out commanding the gates of Hell to open, all attempts to bar the doors prove futile. "Then did the King of glory in his majesty trample upon death, and laid hold on Satan the prince and delivered him unto the power of Hell, and drew Adam to him unto his own brightness."[11] Thus, according to tradition, Adam is the first to be delivered from Hell.

The character of Hell reproaches Satan in words which introduce another aspect of the Descent, the deliberate deceit practiced on a gullible Satan:

[T]hou oughtest first to have sought out matter of evil in this Jesus: Wherefore didst thou adventure without cause to crucify him unjustly against whom thou foundest no blame, and to bring into our realm the innocent and righteous one, and to lose the guilty and the ungodly and unrighteous of the whole world?[12]

In other words, by taking on human form, Christ has caused Satan to overstep his bounds and subsequently lose those in his power.

The Gospel of Nicodemus also indirectly supports the idea of baptism as an essential purpose of the Descent (and hence as a requirement for salvation). Although Christ does not literally baptize those He leads out, He does make the sign of the cross over them.[13] This idea is echoed in another apocryphal work, the Epistle of the Apostles, in which Christ first preaches and then baptizes in Hell in order to ensure fair judgment:

[S]o shall the judgement be accomplished with strictness. . . . For to that end went I down unto the place of Lazarus, and preached unto the righteous and the

---

[10] For a demonstration of the importance of the Harrowing in liturgical texts as well, see Karl Young, *The Harrowing of Hell in Liturgical Drama,* Transactions of the Wisconsin Academy of Sciences, Arts, and Letters, Vol. XVI, Part II, No. 2 (Madison: University of Wisconsin Press, 1909) 889–947.

[11] M. R. James, *The Apocryphal New Testament* (1924; rpt. Oxford: Oxford at the Clarendon Press, 1950) 136. Chapters 17–27 of the Gospel of Nicodemus, "Descensus Christi ad inferos," purport to be the report of two eyewitnesses, the sons of Simeon. Although this document exists in three forms, the majority of manuscripts present "Latin A" (James 118), and its account is followed here except where noted. The first part of the Gospel of Nicodemus, the "Acta Pilati," will not concern us here. Young speculates that these two parts of the Gospel of Nicodemus were written independently, the "Descensus" being an older document (890).

[12] James 137.

[13] James 139.

prophets, that they might come out of the rest which is below and come up into that which is above; and I poured out upon them with my right hand the water of life and forgiveness and salvation from all evil, as I have done unto you and unto them that believe on me.[14]

Ode XLII of the Odes of Solomon, an early second-century work, also refers to Christ's baptism of those that appealed to Him in Hell: "And I heard their voice; / And my name I sealed upon their heads: / For they are free men and they are mine."[15]

Finally, the Gospel of Nicodemus ties up many loose details from the Biblical account, although these matters continued to provide a puzzle for later writers. For example, the gospel explains the fate of Enoch and Elijah, who never suffered death (Enoch was "translated" into heaven for his righteousness, and Elijah was taken to heaven in a chariot of fire); the robber whom Jesus promised would be with Him in Paradise; and those whose graves were opened and their bodies resurrected at the time of the crucifixion (Matthew 27:52–53). The saints, following Christ out of Hell, find Enoch and Elijah waiting for them in Paradise, along with the thief, who had been instructed by the angel at the gate to wait for Adam.[16] The resurrected ones (about 12,000, according to the Latin B version of the gospel)[17] had gone over Jordan for three days, received baptism, and had then risen to Paradise.[18] In addition, the Latin B version introduces the possibility that some saints could have been left behind accidentally during the Harrowing:

Then all the saints of God besought the Lord that he would leave the sign of victory—*even* of the holy cross—in hell, that the wicked ministers thereof might not prevail to keep back any that was accused, whom the Lord absolved. And so it was done, and the Lord set his cross in the midst of hell, which is the sign of victory; and it shall remain there for ever.[19]

Thus both the Bible and the Apocrypha supported the idea of salvation of the Old Testament Fathers, although some question existed as to whether Christ descended to preach to them, deliver them by force, or baptize them.[20] In addition, some question remained as to whether the patriarchs were immediately liberated from Hell or merely promised a future deliverance.

---

[14] James 494.

[15] Quasten 167. The Shepherd of Hermas, however, taught in his *Ninth Similitude* that the apostles and teachers, not Christ, preached and baptized in Hell after their death.

[16] James 141.

[17] James 121.

[18] James 142–143.

[19] James 139. Another possible interpretation is that Christ may pardon sinners in Hell and deliver them by virtue of His cross (a concept which may be applied in the cases of Trajan and the pagan judge of *St. Erkenwald*).

[20] See MacCulloch for a fuller discussion of Biblical (45–56) and Apocryphal (131–173) references to the Descent.

Less sure, however, was the fate of the virtuous classical pagan. Without the Judaic expectation of a Messiah, philosophers and poets had nevertheless attained impressive truths.[21] In addition, all known Christian philosophers from Aristides (136–161) to Clement of Alexandria (ca. 185–211 or 215) were themselves converts from paganism and trained philosophers—and therefore naturally sympathetic to the idea of a philosophized Christianity.[22] But Christianity was not assumed to be the same as philosophy; rather, Christianity was the *fulfillment* of philosophy. Clement describes this relationship between the two:

> For God is the cause of all good things; but of some primarily, as of the Old and New Testament; and of others by consequence, as of philosophy. Perhaps, too, philosophy was given to the Greeks directly and primarily, till the Lord should call the Greeks. For this was a schoolmaster to bring the Greek mind to Christ, as the law brought the Hebrews. Philosophy, therefore, was a preparative, paving the way for him who is perfected in Christ.[23]

This view of the concurrent value of philosophy and Christianity has been labeled the "double faith theory."[24] It was an opinion held by many of the Fathers, most notably Justin, Clement, and Origen, and it evidently disposed them toward a favorable view of the possible salvation of classical thinkers.[25]

Justin was especially interested in the ties between philosophy and Christianity and impressed by the truths of the Platonists, whom he believed to have most nearly approached Christianity. In fact, he supposed Plato to have been influenced by Moses; according to Plato's biographer, he had at one time visited Egypt and had either read a copy of the Pentateuch or had at least made contact with its learned commentators.[26] In addition, Justin felt that salvation was possible for those who had died before the Incarnation: the rational truths attained by men sufficed for their Christianity, since all rational beings share in the universal Logos

---

[21] In this regard, Jean Daniélou's work *Holy Pagans of the Old Testament* (New York: Longmans, Green and Co., 1957) brings out a distinction usually glossed over. The Old Testament speaks of the salvation not only of those under Abraham's covenant but also of those who were not of the tribes of Israel: Abel, Enoch, Daniel, Noah, Job, Melchizedek, Lot, the Queen of Sheba. This would bode well for others outside the Judaeo-Christian realm.

[22] H. A. Wolfson, *Philosophy of the Church Fathers* (Cambridge, Mass.: Harvard University Press, 1970) 11.

[23] *Stromata* 1.5.28.1–3. English translation from Jaroslav Pelikan, *The Emergence of the Catholic Tradition,* Vol. I of *The Christian Tradition: A History of the Development of Doctrine* (Chicago: University of Chicago Press, 1978) 63.

[24] Wolfson 122. The label itself is problematic; although philosophy might point the way to Christianity, it was in no way a substitute for it. The term "double faith" unfortunately implies an equality that the Fathers certainly did not intend.

[25] The likelihood of such salvation was strengthened by the early Church's idea that Christ descended to convert the souls He found in Hell. Of course, this concept also made Christianity more attractive to prospective converts of the early Church by allowing for the salvation of ancestors.

[26] Henry Chadwick, *Early Christian Thought and the Classical Tradition* (New York: Oxford University Press, 1966) 13–14.

or Reason Who is Christ. Thus both Abraham and Socrates were Christians,[27] although those alive before Christ could see the truth only indistinctly.[28]

Clement, as we have seen, likewise acknowledged the imperfect but nevertheless compatible truths of philosophy.[29] Also like Justin, he acknowledged the participation of each man in the Logos, although he did not go so far as to say that this constituted Christianity.[30] He agreed as well on the matter of the probable salvation of Socrates (a model of integrity for Christian martyrs in their resistance of political tyranny) and other Greek philosophers.[31]

Clement was the first to hold that a conversion was produced in Hell by Christ.[32] He asks:

If, then, he [Christ] preached the gospel to those in the flesh in order that they might not be condemned unjustly, how is it conceivable that he did not for the same reason preach the gospel to those who had departed this life before his coming?[33]

As a secondary point, he introduces the possibility that Christ may have preached only to the Jewish souls and left the others for the apostles, a concept based on a passage in the Shepherd of Hermas.[34]

Clement's pupil, Origen, concurred with the belief that through the exercise of reason man participates in the eternal reason of God and thus attains truth.[35] In his *Contra Celsum,* replying to Celsus' charge that Christians have nothing new to contribute compared to classical philosophy, Origen uses this argument in favor of Christianity. Since every man has an innate awareness of truth, the congruity of philosophy and Christianity confirms the truth of the Christians. At the same time, however, Origen asserts the necessity of salvation through Christ; natural morality is not

[27] *Apologia* I, 46. From Chadwick 16.

[28] *Apologia* II, 13. From S. Harent, "Infidèles—Salut des," *Dictionnaire de Théologie Catholique,* Vol. VII, col. 1808.

[29] See also his appeal to his philosophical colleagues to complete their world view by accepting Christ: "That which the chief of philosophy only guessed at, the disciples of Christ have both apprehended and proclaimed." *Protrepticus,* II. 112.2. English translation from Pelikan, Vol. I, 46.

[30] See *Stromateis* V. 133, 8–9; I. 10.4; *Protrepticus* 117. From Chadwick 39.

[31] *Stromateis* V. 133–134, 141. From Chadwick 45. Socrates' fate became a popular topic in the Middle Ages, acquiring many fanciful accretions to bring Socrates within the pale of Christianity. A. J. Minnis (*Chaucer and Pagan Antiquity* [Totowa, N.J.: Rowman and Littlefield, 1982] 51) summarizes the treatment of Socrates by William of Conches, William of Aragon, Nicholas Trevet, and Jean de Meun.

[32] *Stromata* VI, vi. From Harent, "Infidèles," col. 1814.

[33] *Patrologia Graeca* (hereafter referred to as *P.G.*), Vol. 9, lib. VI, cap. vi, col. 274C. English translation from R.V. Turner, "*Descendit ad inferos:* Medieval Views on Christ's Descent Into Hell and the Salvation of the Ancient Just," *Journal of the History of Ideas* 27 (1966): 174.

[34] Harent, col. 1815.

[35] *De Principiis* I.1,1. From William A. Banner, "Origen and the Tradition of Natural Law Concepts" in *Dumbarton Oaks Papers* 8 (Cambridge, Mass.: Harvard University Press, 1954) 73.

enough.[36] Therefore, Origen agrees with Clement's belief that Christ's descent was made to convert souls in Hades:

[W]hen he became a soul unclothed by a body he conversed with souls unclothed by bodies, also converting those of them who were willing to accept him, or those who, for reasons which he himself knew, he saw to be ready to do so.[37]

Both Clement and Origen differed from the traditional view of Hell and maintained the Neoplatonic doctrine of the purification of souls and their eventual reunion with God. Origen states:

The process of purification and instruction begun on earth is continued after death. The good, clothed in a refined spiritual body, enter 'paradise,' or 'a certain place of education, an auditorium or school of souls.' Now are solved for the spirit all the problems which have been presented here in nature, history, and faith.[38]

This belief was one of several that eventually led to the condemnation of Origen as a heretic, for in 229 Origen disputed at Athens with Candidus on the related point of Satan's salvation (apocatastasis). Origen contended that the devil fell through his will, not his nature, and therefore even his redemption was possible.[39]

Thus these three Fathers—Justin, Clement, and Origen—all applauded the confluence of philosophy and Christianity.[40] The early Fathers did not, however, hold philosophy equal to Christianity, nor did they hold all philosophers equal. Platonism seemed most congenial to Christianity. But Epicureans had been questioned as atheists even by pagan philosophers, Stoics did not concede the incorporeality and providence of God, and Aristotle was held as an excellent guide on the terrestrial level but unreliable otherwise.[41] Even in the case of Platonism, the Church Fathers held philosophy as the mere handmaiden of faith, a relationship symbolized by the figures of Hagar and Sarah.[42]

Not all Church Fathers, though, conceded the value of philosophy or the salvation of the classical philosophers. Opposed to the "double faith"

---

[36] De Principiis III.1.17; Contra Celsum III. 81. From Chadwick 105.

[37] P.G., Vol. XI, lib. II, cap. xliii, col. 863–866. English translation from Henry Chadwick's Origen: Contra Celsum (Cambridge: Cambridge University Press, 1953) 99–100.

[38] De Principiis II,11,4,5. English translation from Reinhold Seeberg, Text-Book of the History of Doctrines, trans. Charles E. Hay (Grand Rapids, Michigan: Baker Book House, 1952) I, 159.

[39] Chadwick, Early Christian Thought 99. Apocatastasis was condemned during the Second Council of Constantinople in 553, and until the sixteenth century the prevalent stress was on the punitive purpose of God's judgment. For more information on the subject of apocatastasis, see C. A. Patrides, "Salvation of Satan," Journal of the History of Ideas 28 (1967): 467–478.

[40] Daniélou goes so far as to affirm that this was "the attitude of all the first Christian writers" (Holy Pagans 19). It would be more accurate to say that the majority of the Fathers recognized in the teachings of philosophy a revelation similar to that of the Old Testament as a preparation for Christianity.

[41] Wolfson 84–89. On the medieval issue of Aristotle's salvation, see A.H. Chroust, "Contribution to the Medieval Discussion: 'utrum Aristoteles sit salvatus,'" Journal of the History of Ideas 6 (1945): 231–238.

[42] Wolfson 97.

theory acknowledging the merit of philosophy was that of "single faith," expressed most forcefully by Tertullian. To him, faith unadorned by reason is best, as illustrated in two often-quoted comments: "What has Athens to do with Jerusalem?"[43] and "I believe it because it is absurd."[44] Not surprisingly, Tertullian denied that classical philosophers had attained Christian truth. Using Socrates as an example, he asserts:

It is therefore not to be wondered at, if even in his person . . . he, in the face of death itself, asserts the immortality of the soul by a strong assumption such as was wanted to frustrate the wrong [they had inflicted upon him]. So that all the wisdom of Socrates, at that moment, proceeded from the affectation of an assumed composure, rather than the firm conviction of ascertained truth. For by whom has truth ever been discovered without God?[45]

Tertullian did concur with Clement's and Origen's teachings on the purpose of the Descent, although (as we might expect) he restricted those who were converted by Christ: "Nor did he ascend into the heights of heaven before descending into the lower parts of the earth, that He might there make the patriarchs and prophets partakers of Himself."[46]

In the late fourth and early fifth centuries, Augustine reversed the emphasis of the early Church on Christ's conversion of the souls He found in Hell. At the same time, he sanctioned the Judaic idea of a bi-level Hell with different degrees of suffering and retained many of the earlier patristic opinions. For example, he asserted the value of philosophy, which contains truths Christians may accept:

Philosophi autem qui vocantur, si qua forte vera et fidei nostrae accommodata dixerunt, maxime Platonici, non solum formidanda non sunt, sed ab eis etiam tanquam injustis possessoribus in usum nostrum vindicanda.[47]

He accepted the possibility of salvation for those alive before the Incarnation—not, however, through the truths of philosophy, but through faith in the coming Saviour:

---

[43] *De Praescriptione Haereticorum* 7; *Apologeticus* 46. English translation from Chadwick, *Early Christian Thought* 1.

[44] *De Carne Christi* 5. English translation from Chadwick, *Early Christian Thought* 2. This attitude in some ways parallels that of gnosticism, a belief condemned as heretical because of its teaching of pure revelation of the elect and total depravity of the damned, with no criteria of rational judgment (Chadwick 9). The gnostic Marcion, according to Irenaeus, went so far as to assert that Christ descended to save Cain, Esau, and all who had turned away from the God of the Jews and had left behind Abel, Enoch, Noah, Abraham, Isaac, Jacob, Moses, David, and Solomon (Harent, "Infidèles," col. 1819; see also MacCulloch 300–311).

[45] Tertullian, *De Anima,* in *The Writings of Tertullian,* Vol. II. Vol. XV in the Ante-Nicene Christian Library, ed. Rev. Alexander Roberts and James Donaldson (Edinburgh: T. and T. Clark, 1870) 411–412.

[46] Tertullian 530. Although this passage is open to interpretation, Constance I. Smith ("Reply to '*Descendit ad inferos*: Medieval Views on Christ's Descent Into Hell and the Salvation of the Ancient Just,'" *Journal of the History of Ideas* 30 [1969]: 250) reads it as a eucharistic reference, an idea also expressed in the twelfth century by Rupert of Deutz.

[47] *De doctrina christiana II. P.L.,* Vol. 34, cap. XL, col. 63.

Sacramentum porro regenerationis nostrae manifestum esse voluit manifestatus Mediator. Erat autem antiquis justis aliquod occultum, cum tamen et illi eadem fide salvi fierent, quae fuerat suo tempore revelanda. Non enim audemus fideles temporis nostri praeferre amicis Dei per quos nobis ista prophetata sunt, cum Deum Abraham et Deum Isaac et Deum Jacob, ita se Deus esse commendet, ut hoc dicat suum nomen in aeternum (*Exod.* iii, 15). Quod si circumcisio antiquis sanctis pro Baptismo fuisse creditur, quid respondebitur de his qui antequam hoc praeceptum esset, Deo placuerent, non tamen sine fide?.... Sicut autem illi, quando idem Sacramentum occultum erat, credebant Christi incarnationem futuram, sic et nos credimus factam: et a nobis autem et ab illis futurus exspectatur ad judicium ejus adventus.[48]

On the matter of the Descent itself, Augustine evidences some confusion. In his sermons on the Creed, he states that Christ descended to free Adam, the patriarchs and prophets, and all the just who were guilty only of original sin:

Descendit ad inferna, ut Adam protoplastum, et Patriarchas, et Prophetas, omnesque justos, qui pro originali peccato ibidem destinebantur, liberaret; et ut de vinculis peccati absolutos, de eadem captivitate et inferni loco, suo sanguine redemptos, ad supernam patriam et ad perpetuae vitae guadia revocaret. Reliqui qui supra originale peccatum principalem culpam commiserunt, ut asserit Scriptura, in poenali tartaro remanserunt, sicut in persona Christi dictum est per prophetam, *Ero mors tua, o mors;* id est, morte sua Christus humani generis inimicam mortem interfecit, et vitam dedit. *Ero morsus tuus, inferni* (*Osee* xiii, 14). Partim momordit infernum pro parte eorum quos liberavit: partim reliquit, pro parte eorum qui pro principalibus criminibus in tormentis remanserunt.[49]

Further, he postulates two regions in Hell: a lower region where the damned are punished and the resting place of the just, the "bosom of Abraham" or "paradise" (from the story of the beggar Lazarus and the rich man in Luke 16:19–31 and from Christ's words to the repentant thief on the cross in Luke 23:43).[50]

However, in a letter to Bishop Evodius answering his questions about I Peter 3:18–20, Augustine contradicts himself and denies that the bosom

---

[48] *De Praesentia Dei Liber, seu Epistola CLXXXVII. P.L.,* Vol. 33, cap. II, col. 845–846.

[49] *Sermo de Symbolo. P.L.,* Vol. 40, cap. VII, col. 1194.

[50] *De Praesentia Dei Liber, seu Epistola CLXXXVII. P. L.,* Vol. 33, cap. II, col. 834:

Si ergo secundum hominem quem Verbum Deus suscepit, putamus dictum esse, *Hodie mecum eris in paradiso,* non ex his verbis in coelo existimandus est esse paradisus: neque enim ipso die in coelo futurus erat homo Christus Jesus; sed in inferno secundum animum, in sepulcro autem secundum carnem.... Restat igitur ut, si secundum hominem dictum est, *Hodie mecum eris in paradiso,* in inferno intelligatur esse paradisus, ubi erat eo die futurus secundum humanam animam Christus. Utrum autem sinus ille Abrahae, ubi dives impius cum in tormentis esset inferni, requiescentem pauperem vidit, vel paradisi consendus vocabulo, vel ad inferos pertinere existimandus sit, non facile dixerim. De illo quippe divite legimus dictum esse, *Mortuus est autem et dives, et sepultus est in inferno;* et, *cum apud inferos in tormentis esset.* In pauperis autem morte vel requie non sunt inferi nominati; sed, *Contigit,* inquit, *mori inopem illum, et auferri ab Angelis in sinum Abrahae.* Deinde ardenti diviti dicit Abraham, *Inter nos et vos chaos magnum firmatum est* (Luc. xvi, 22–26): tanquam inter inferos sedesque beatorum.

of Abraham formed part of Hell.[51] This puts him in perplexity, then, about why Christ descended into Hell, as Scripture (in his view) clearly states. He is forced by church tradition to believe that Christ freed Adam from Hell,[52] and it seems certain that He must have saved others as well, but he cannot conjecture whom:

Sed quia evidentia testimonia et infernum commemorant et dolores, nulla causa occurrit cur ille credatur venisse Salvator, nisi ut ab ejus doloribus salvos faceret; sed utrum omnes quos in eis invenit, an quosdam quos illo beneficio dignos judicavit, adhuc requiro.[53]

In contrast to the early Fathers, though, Augustine was sure that Christ did not preach to those in Hell, and that those after the Resurrection lacking knowledge of the Gospel would not have the opportunity of salvation by hearing of Christ in Hell. This would lead to the bizarre conclusion that the Gospel should *not* be preached so that all could be saved after death:

aliud sequitur absurdius, ut hic non sit Evangelium praedicandum, quoniam omnes utique morituri sunt, et sine ullo reatu contempti Evangelii venire ad inferos debent, ut eis prodesse possit, cum ibi crediderint: quod sentire, impiae vanitatis est.[54]

At the same time, he realized the attractiveness of believing that Christ freed all he found in Hell, especially those classical writers admired by himself and his contemporaries. But this cannot be, since their good acts were futilely directed toward human glory rather than devotion to God:

Si enim omnes omnino dixerimus tunc esse liberatos, qui illic inventi sunt, quis non gratuletur, si hoc possimus ostendere? praesertim propter quosdam qui nobis litterario labore suo familiariter innotuerunt, quorum eloquium ingeniumque mir-amur; non solum poetas et oratores, qui . . . aliquando etiam unum Deum verumque

---

[51] *Epistola CLXIV. P.L.,* Vol. 33, cap. III, col. 711:

Sed quonam modo intelligatur Abraham, in cujus sinum pius etiam pauper ille susceptus est, in illis fuisse doloribus, ego quidem non video. . . . Quanquam in his ipsis tanti magistri verbis, ubi ait dixisse Abraham, *Inter vos et nos chaos magnum firmatum est,* satis, ut opinor, appareat non esse quamdam partem, et quasi membrum inferorum, tantae illius felicitatis sinum.

[52] *P.L.,* Vol. 33, cap. III, col. 711:

Et de illo quidem primo homine patre generis humani, quod eum inde solverit, Ecclesia fere tota consentit; quod eam non inaniter credidisse credendum est, undecumque hoc traditum sit, etiamsi canonicarum Scripturarum hinc expressa non proferatur auctoritas.

[53] *P.L.,* Vol. 33, col. 711.

[54] *P.L.,* Vol. 33, col. 714. See J. Wang Tch'ang-Tche, *Saint Augustin et les vertus des paiens* (Paris: Gabriel Beauchesne et ses fils, 1938), for an analysis of Augustine's teachings on the issue of pagan salvation. Wang points out that Augustine was forced to take a harsh stance in order to counter the Pelagians' claim that human nature alone, without benefit of grace, could fulfill divine law and merit salvation (75–79, 104). For Augustine, true virtue was inevitably linked to Christian revelation. But in Tch'ang-Tche's final chapter (141–182), he demonstrates that Augustine does not *oblige* us to refuse to pagans the possession of true virtue or the hope of salvation; the difficulty lies in how to explain the manner in which a pagan could receive Christian faith.

confessi sunt ... verum etiam illos qui haec non cantando vel declamando, sed philosophando dixerunt: multos etiam quorum litteras non habemus, sed in illorum litteris didicimus secundum quemdam modum laudabiles vitas. ... Quae quidem omnia quando non referuntur ad finem rectae veraeque pietatis, sed ad fastum inanem humanae laudis et gloriae, etiam ipsa inanescunt quodammodo, steriliaque redduntur.[55]

In the same letter, Augustine radically alters the traditional gloss of I Peter 3:18–20, which states that Christ preached to the "spirits in prison"—the men of Noah's time, who were generally assumed to be suffering in Hell.[56] Since he did not believe that Christ descended to convert souls, Augustine decided that Peter was speaking not of the period after Christ's death but using the time of the Deluge as an analogy to that following Christ's ascension. Thus those who refuse to believe in the Gospel during the construction of the Church (the ark) are the spirits in prison, shut up in ignorance. And as Noah and his family were saved by water, so believers are saved by baptism.[57] In effect, then, Augustine denied a literal interpretation of this passage. Although the East did not accept this view, Western theologians did throughout the Middle Ages.[58]

In explaining this passage, Augustine again shows his confusion by contradicting himself. Although he had earlier seemed to deny salvation to the pagan philosophers, here he asserts that from the beginning of the human race Christ has been on earth in the spirit if not in the flesh, so that some believed to their salvation. He apparently has the people of the Old Testament in mind, but he does not exclude others. Thus Christ came "vel ad consolandos bonos, vel ad utrosque admonendos, ut alii ad

---

[55] *P.L.,* Vol. 33, col. 710.

[56] H. Quilliet, "Descente de Jésus aux enfers," *Dictionnaire de Théologie Catholique,* Vol. IV, col. 591. The verses are as follows in the King James version:

For Christ also hath once suffered for sins, the just for the unjust, that he might bring us to God, being put to death in the flesh, but quickened by the Spirit:

By which also he went and preached unto the spirits in prison;

Which sometime were disobedient, when once the longsuffering of God waited in the days of Noah, while the ark was a preparing, wherein few, that is, eight souls were saved by water.

The Vulgate version reads: "Quia et Christus semel pro peccatis nostris mortuus est, iustus pro iniustis, ut non offerret Deo, mortificatus quidem carne, vivificatus autem spiritu. / In quo et his qui in carcere erant spiritibus veniens praedicavit, / qui increduli fuerant aliquando, quando expectabant Dei patientiam in diebus Noe cum fabricaretur arca, in qua pauci, id est octo animae salvae factae sunt per aquam."

[57] *P.L.,* Vol. 33, col. 715:

Considera tamen ne forte totum illud quod de conclusis in carcere spiritibus, qui in diebus Noe non crediderant, Petrus apostolus dicit, omnino ad inferos non pertineat, sed ad illa potius tempora quorum formam ad haec tempora transtulit ... ut ii qui modo non credunt Evangelio, dum in omnibus gentibus aedificatur Ecclesia, illis intelligantur esse similes, qui tunc non crediderunt cum fabricaretur arca: illi autem qui crediderunt, et per Baptismum salvi fiunt, illis comparentur, qui tunc in eadem arca salvi facti sunt per aquam.

[58] Quilliet, cols. 593–594.

salutem suam crederent, alii ad poenam suam non crederent, ipse utique non in carne, sed in spiritu veniebat."[59]

From this short summary, we can see that Augustine was (as indeed he admitted to Evodius) unclear about many points relating to Christ's descent. Overall, this matter seemed beyond human comprehension: "Quod si de omnibus acceperimus, manet quaestio, quare Petrus eos tantum commemoravit, qui tunc increduli fuerunt cum fabricaretur arca."[60] However, Augustine definitely ruled out the earlier concept of conversion in Hell and accepted instead the idea of divisions in Hell.

Augustine's views were generally upheld by Gregory the Great in the sixth century. Like Augustine, he taught that the Hebrew Fathers were saved by their expectation of a Messiah. (He did not, however, ascribe merit to philosophical truth as Augustine had; he contended that faith which is supported by reason has no merit.[61]) He used the description of Jesus' triumphal entry into Jerusalem to illustrate the salvation of those before the Incarnation:

Sed qui praeibant et qui sequebantur clamabant: Hosanna. Praecessit quippe Judaicus populus, secutus est gentilis. . . . Hosanna autem Latina lingua, salva nos dicitur. Ab ipso enim salutem et priores quaesierunt, et praesentes quaerunt; et benedictum qui venit in nomine Domini confitentur, quoniam una spes, una fides est praecedentium atque sequentium populorum. Nam sicut illi exspectata passione ac resurrectione ejus sanati sunt, ita nos praeterita passione illius ac permanente in saecula resurrectione salvamur.[62]

Also like Augustine, Gregory firmly rejected the notion that Christ descended into Hell to preach there. In his *Epistola XV, Ad Georgium Presbyterum,* he reproved two officers of the church at Constantinople for teaching that Christ released from Hell all who acknowledged Him as God. He informed them that Christ released only those who in their fleshly existence had exercised faith and (as an addition to Augustine's teaching) good works: "descendens ad inferos Dominus illos solummodo ab inferni claustris eripuit quos viventes in carne per suam gratiam in fide et bona operatione servavit."[63] Whether this criterion included pagans as well as Jews is left uncertain.

In summary, then, we see that Christ's descent into Hell was accepted by many of the Church Fathers. (One notable exception was John Chrysostom, who believed that Christ's breaking down the doors of Hell signified His triumph over death, nothing else.[64]) Although not all agreed with them, Clement and Origen were influential in teaching that Christ (or His apostles) descended to Hell to preach to those who had died before

---

[59] *P.L.,* Vol. 33, cap. VI, col. 716.

[60] *Epistola CLXIV. P.L.,* Vol. 33, cap. IV, col. 713.

[61] "Nec fides habet meritum, cui humana ratio praebet experimentum." *Homil. in Evang. XXVI. P.L.,* Vol. 76, col. 1197C.

[62] *Homilium in Ezechielem,* lib. II. *P.L.,* Vol. 76, cols. 985C-986A.

[63] *P.L.,* Vol. 77, cols. 869B-870C.

[64] Harent, col. 1817.

the Incarnation. This left the door open for universal salvation, so that the classical philosophers these theologians admired could be admitted to heaven; made the new religion more palatable to its converts, since their deceased loved ones had been offered the opportunity for salvation; and generally reflected the prominent concern of the early Church, conversion. For the most part, Augustine's views on the Descent were accepted as authoritative by the later Church: Christ did not descend to convert, but He had liberated souls from Hell. To understand His timing or His choice, however, was beyond man's domain. From this standpoint we turn to the re-opening of the issue in the twelfth century.

The Middle Ages—Twelfth and Thirteenth Centuries

In the twelfth century, a revival of interest in the ancient Greeks and Romans led to a revival of the debate over their spiritual fate. During this century and the next, the Descent itself was generally accepted, although Abelard questioned it as a literal happening and imparted to the crucifixion itself a controversial meaning.[65] The primary focus of interest, however, was on identification of those who had been freed from Hell. As in the early Church, theologians tended to divide between those who saw value in philosophical truth and those who did not. Proponents of faith alone were more likely to believe that Christ descended to liberate the Old Testament Jews who had anticipated the coming of a Saviour. These more conservative theologians (although not all denied the value of philosophy) included Bernard of Clairvaux, Peter the Lombard, Hugh of St. Victor, and Alain of Lille. On the other hand, two men who markedly stressed the value of man's reason extended the possibility of salvation to pagans as well. Abelard and Aquinas (followed by the comparatively minor Alexander of Hales) led the way to the formula "facere quod in se est" (to those who did their best, God would not withhold grace),

---

[65] See pp. 24–25 for a discussion of Abelard's view of the Descent. Abelard was also instrumental in imparting a new meaning to Christ's crucifixion, which had undergone a changing interpretation through the years. Using the analogy of Greek and Roman slaves who purchased their freedom, Paul had declared that by Christ's blood we were freed from sin. Irenaeus, Origen, Basil, Gregory of Nyssa, and Ambrose elaborated on this view to explain the redemption as a ransom due the devil (Quilliet, "Descente," col. 603). From this idea the concept of outwitting the devil developed. The "Ransom Theory" was accepted by Augustine and remained authoritative for almost a thousand years. Anselm of Canterbury modified this view in the eleventh century. He saw Christ's death not as a payment due the devil but due God, whose majesty had been injured by Adam's sin (Cur Deus Homo? I. 7; P.L., Vol. 158, cols. 367ff; also Medit. XI, col. 764). Abelard used Anselm's arguments but did not see Christ's death as payment of righteousness: "True charity would no longer be afraid to endure anything for his sake" ("nil jam tolerare ipsum vera reformidet charitas"; Epist. ad Romanos, II. 3; P.L., Vol. 178, col. 836B). Against Abelard's exemplarist theory, Bernard of Clairvaux defended the traditional view of Christ's death as a ransom for man:

Non requisivit Deus Pater sanguinem Filii, sed tamen acceptavit oblatum; non sanguinem sitiens, sed salutem, quia salus erat in sanguine. Salus plane, et non, sicut iste [Abelard] sapit et scribit, sola charitatis ostensio. (Contra Quaedam Capitula Errorum Abelardi; P.L., Vol. 182, cap. xxii, col. 1070C).

which would play an important role in fourteenth-century thinking. Another development of twelfth- and thirteenth-century thought was a greater interest in the "waiting room" of paradise. Whether it contained only Jews or the just pagans as well, hypotheses were advanced as to its location and the conditions there.

Let us turn now to a more detailed examination of these points, beginning with those theologians who upheld the position that, since faith was a prerequisite for salvation, only the Old Testament patriarchs were liberated from Hell at Christ's descent.

Bernard of Clairvaux strongly advocated the belief that faith should be unsupported by miracles or by attempts to demonstrate its rationality: "Faith is a voluntary and certain foretaste of truth which has not yet been made manifest" ("Fides est voluntaria quaedam et certa praelibatio necdum propalatae veritatis").[66] Bernard's method of conversion has been characterized as rhetorical, not intellectual.[67] Therefore, he overtly attacked his contemporary Abelard for his boldness in applying his mind to anything on heaven or on earth: "Qui dum omnium quae sunt in coelo sursum, et quae in terra deorsum, nihil, praeter solum Nescio, nescire dignatur."[68] In the same vein, Bernard writes:

Irridetur simplicium fides, eviscerantur arcana Dei, quaestiones de altissimis rebus temerarie ventilantur, insultatur patribus, quod eas magis sopiendas, quam solvendas censuerint. . . . Ita omnia usurpat sibi humanum ingenium, fidei nil reservans.[69]

In his teaching on the Song of Songs, though, he made clear his stand. He was not opposed to reason and to learning, but they were not necessary for salvation. Thus for Bernard reason and faith are two separate entities, not complementary.[70]

But Bernard was convinced of the salvation of those who had believed in Christ's coming even before the Incarnation.[71] They waited in Abraham's bosom, safe from the tortures of Hell, as Bernard asserts in answer to a question posed by Abelard:

Deinde infert: "Nunquid etiam pauperem illum, qui in sinu Abrahae requiescebat, sicut et divitem damnatum, diabolus cruciabat; aut etiam in ipsum Abraham dominium habebat, caeterosque electos?" Non: sed habuisset, si non liberati fuissent fide venturi. . . . Propterea jam tunc sanguis Christi rorabat enim Lazaro ne flammas sentiret: quod et ipse credidisset in eum qui erat passurus. Sic de omnibus electis illius temporis sentiendum, natos quidem et ipsos, aeque ut nos, sub po-

---

[66] *De Consid.* v. 3.6. *P.L.,* Vol. 182, col. 791A.
[67] J. G. Sikes, *Peter Abailard* (Cambridge: Cambridge University Press, 1932) 35.
[68] *Contra Quaedam Capitula Errorum Abelardi,* 1, 1. *P.L.,* Vol. 182, col. 1055A.
[69] *Epistola CLXXXVIII. P.L.,* Vol. 182, col. 353A.
[70] *Sermones in Cantica,* Sermo xxxvi. *P.L.,* Vol. 183, col. 967C: "quantos enumerat Apostolus in Epistola ad Hebraeos, factos dilectos, non in scientiam litterarum, sed in conscientia pura et fide non ficta (*Hebr.* xl). Omnes placuerunt Deo in vita sua, vitae meritis, non scientiae."
[71] *Epistola Seu Tractatus, De Baptismo . . . P.L.,* Vol. 182, col. 1041A.

testate tenebrarum, propter originale peccatum: sed erutos antequam morerentur, et nonnisi in sanguine Christi.[72]

Those who waited in Abraham's bosom enjoyed a place of quiet and refreshment, separated from the punishment of Hell, until Christ led them from this region to the throne of heaven.[73] Although Bernard does not explicitly discuss the fate of the classical pagans, we can assume that he would not credit their philosophical systems with the ability to reach Christian truth.

Peter Lombard followed in Bernard's steps on the subject of Christ's descent and its implications for the salvation of pagans. His *Quatuor Libri Sententiarum,* a collection of questions about Christian beliefs with quotes from pertinent authorities, became a seminal work for the medieval period.[74] Under the heading "De fide antiquorum," he discusses the necessity of belief in a Mediator for those living both before and after the Incarnation:

Est autem quaedam fidei mensura, sine qua nunquam potuit esse salus .... nec ante adventum, nec ante legem videtur hoc suffecisse, quia sine fide Mediatoris nullum hominem, vel ante, vel post, fuisse salvum sanctorum auctoritates contestantur.[75]

This belief, however, was not the same for all. The prophets possessed a clear understanding; the masses of people had a "veiled" faith, accepting the teachings of their leaders as contemporary Christians accept the Creed without understanding it:

Dici potest nullum fuisse justum vel salvum cui non esset facta revelatio vel distincta, vel velata, vel in aperto, vel in mysterio. Distincta, ut Abrahae et Moysi, aliisque majoribus, qui distinctionem articulorum fidei habebant; velata, ut simplicibus quibus revelatum erat ea esse credenda, quae credebant illi majores et docebant, sed eorum distinctionem apertam non habebant.[76]

Thus for the Lombard, understanding and faith are separate capacities, understanding being a dispensable element unnecessary for salvation.

To prove that faith in Christ, though, was an absolute prerequisite for salvation, the Lombard uses the illustration of Cornelius, the centurion

---

[72] *Contra Quaedam Capitula Errorum Abelardi. P.L.,* Vol. 182, cap. vii, col. 1068AB.

[73] *Sermo IV, De sinu Abrahae. P.L.,* Vol. 183, col. 472AB:

[S]ed providerat eis Dominus in inferno ipso locum quietis et refrigerii, chaos magnum firmans inter sanctas illas animas, et animas impiorum. Quamvis enim utraeque in tenebris essent, non utraeque erant in poenis; sed cruciabantur impii, justi vero consolabantur.... Hunc ergo locum, obscurum quidem, sed quietum, sinum Abrahae Dominus vocat.... In hunc ergo locum Salvator descendens contrivit portas aereas, et vectes ferreos confregit, eductosque vinctos de domo carceris, sedentes quidem, hoc est quiescentes, sed in tenebris et umbra mortis, jam tunc quidem sub altare Dei collocavit.

[74] Students who intended to attain a mastership in theology spent an entire year preparing lectures (delivered the following year) on this work. Thus the views of Peter Lombard are those officially sanctioned by the Church.

[75] *Sententiarum,* Lib. IV, dist. xxv, *De fide antiquorum. P.L.,* Vol. 192, col. 809.

[76] *P.L.,* Vol. 192, cols. 809–810.

in Acts 10. He believed in one God and the coming of the Saviour, but he did not know whether this Saviour had yet come. Pleased with his faith, God sent St. Peter to instruct Cornelius in the details of Christ's coming. Peter Lombard concludes:

Sed si posset sine fide Christi esse salus, non ad eum mitteretur architectus Ecclesiae Petrus. Attende quid ait, sine fide Christi non posse esse salutem; et tamen Cornelium exauditum antequam crederet in Christum. Quod ita potest intelligi, scilicet antequam sciret Christum incarnatum, in quem credebat in mysterio.[77]

This story, then, demonstrates the possibility of direct revelation for those who please God by their faith, despite their imperfect knowledge of the details of that faith.

Hugh of St. Victor basically agrees with the Lombard's views; those born before Christ merited salvation through faith in the Saviour to come, although they did not actually understand this belief:

Sic ergo intelligendum putamus quod dicit beatus Augustinus, quod eadem fides mediatoris salvos justos faciebat antiquos, pusillos cum magnis. . . . Alii quidem quae ventura erant, sicut ventura credentes et cognoscentes; alii vero non quidem cognoscentes, sed credendo et desiderando, cognoscentibus et credentibus adhaerentes.[78]

Likewise, it was possible for the ancient just to partake of the sacraments, although again not all could penetrate their symbolic meaning:

[I]n ipsis eamdem redemptionem suam, quasi in umbra et figura portaverunt . . . . sacramenta passionis ejus, omnes quidem per fidem portaverunt, sed non omnes per cognitionem, quod portaverunt intelligere meruerunt.[79]

Alain of Lille's *De Fide Catholica: Contra Haereticos, Valdenses, Iudaeos et Paganos* was a completely different type of work from the Lombard's textbook. Composed between 1185 and 1200, it seems to have been designed as a systematic handbook in which the user could look up refutations of points raised by heretics.[80] Each group is treated separately in a book of its own, so the presentation of the doctrine of the Descent receives different emphasis in each book. Alain believes that in earlier times the use of reason could lead heretics to Christ; at the time of his writing, however, heretics (specifically, the Albigensians) had let their imaginations run unbounded by reason, not recognizing that their perceptions are limited by their senses:

[T]amen propter novos haereticos novis, imo veteribus et novissimis haeresibus debacchantes, philosophicis speculationibus deditos, sed sensuum speculis destinatos; cogor disertis rationibus de fide rationabili reddere rationem, qui in hoc ab

---

[77] *P.L.,* Vol. 192, col. 810.

[78] *De Sacramentis,* Lib. I, Pars X, cap. vii. *P.L.,* Vol. 176, col. 340AB.

[79] *P.L.,* Vol. 176, col. 340CD.

[80] G. R. Evans, *Alan of Lille, The Frontiers of Theology in the Later Twelfth Century* (Cambridge: Cambridge University Press, 1983) 117.

antiquis haereticis differunt, quod illi humanis rationibus fidem nostram expugnare conati sunt; isti vero nulla ratione humana vel divina freti, ad voluntatem et voluptatem suam, monstruosa confingunt.[81]

Alain alternates reason with authority so that the user of his book can employ whichever form of proof is appropriate in a particular case. Since the heretics he addresses accept some authorities, he primarily restricts himself to these and explains how they have been misinterpreted.[82]

In the first book, Alain outlines one heretical belief of the Albigensians: they deny Christ's descent into Hell and teach that all those in Hell (among whom they include John the Baptist) will remain there eternally:

Dicunt etiam Christum ad inferos non descendisse, nec animas ab inferno liberasse; quia asserunt animas omnium illorum qui ante adventum Christi decesserunt, aeternaliter damnatas esse . . . . dicunt Joannem Baptismam ideo damnatum, quia dubitavit de adventu Christi ad infernum.[83]

Alain refutes their view by citing passages from the New Testament, which the Albigensians accepted, proving that John the Baptist recognized Christ as Saviour.[84] Indeed, "Ipse etiam in utero matris exsultavit in adventu Virginis."[85] He quotes passages which point to Christ's descent into Hell (Luke 11:21–22 and Ephesians 4:8–9), includes the formula "Descendit ad inferos" from the Creed, and asks, "Sed si descendit ad inferos, ad quid descendit, nisi ut captivos liberaret? non enim gratia sui meriti descendit, sed ad liberandum eos quos diabolus in inferno injuste detinebat."[86] Further, he asserts that those who were freed did not go to the earthly paradise, for this is a corporeal rather than a spiritual region.[87]

Later in Book I, Alain must counter the heretics' belief that the Old Testament Fathers deserved eternal punishment for their sins, which he enumerates. Even Enoch, in their argument, is damned because of his enormous sins.[88] Alain begins with the general argument that the Mosaic law was good because it came from God and that those who fulfilled it with love merited eternal life: "lex Mosaica a Deo data fuit, et bona, ita illi qui eam ex charitate impleverunt, vitam aeternam meruerunt."[89] He then presents verses of Scripture which prove the goodness of Moses, Abraham, Jacob, Noah, Enoch, and the other patriarchs.[90] Incidentally, he mentions his belief about the nature of Abraham's bosom ("per sinum

---

[81] *De Fide Catholica . . .* , *Prologus. P.L.*, Vol. 210, col. 307AB.

[82] Evans 131–132. Evans points out that Aquinas likewise recognizes the division between reason and authority. But since he is addressing the pagan, not the heretic, in his *Summa Contra Gentiles,* he begins with reason and works his way up to the authorities.

[83] *P.L.,* Vol. 210, cap. xv, col. 319B.

[84] *P.L.,* Vol. 210, cap. xvi, col. 319C.

[85] *P.L.,* Vol. 210, cap. xvi, col. 319D.

[86] *P.L.,* Vol. 210, col. 320AB.

[87] *P.L.,* Vol. 210, col. 320C.

[88] *P.L.,* Vol. 210, cap. xxxvii, cols. 341B–342B.

[89] *P.L.,* Vol. 210, cap. xxxviii, col. 342B.

[90] *P.L.,* Vol. 210, cols. 342B–344D.

Abrahae intelligitur requies") and the existence of an intermediate waiting place for the blessed ("Enoch . . . in paradisum terrestrem aut alium locum nobis occultum, a Deo ductus est").[91] More important, he implies that ignorance ameliorates wrongdoing, so that some otherwise shameful acts should not be held against the patriarchs: "Si Noe vini virtutem ignorans, inebriatus est, quae culpa in eo?"[92]

Thus Alain concludes that the Old Testament Fathers descended to Hell not for their sins, as the Albigensians wrongly believed, but because of original sin. But, like St. Bernard, Alain feels that they were not actually punished and that they did not descend to the lowest regions of Hell: "Ad horum quoque in infernum descendebant, ubi non puniebantur materiali poena, sed carentia visionis Dei, felici spe consolati; nec ad profundum inferni descendebat."[93] This meant that Christ did not free all those ensnared in Hell; those who did not fulfill the Mosaic law were left behind:

Mortuus enim est ut eos qui detinebantur in tenebris pro effectu peccati originalis, liberaret. . . . In hoc omnes, secundum Apostolum, maledicto legis fuerunt subjecti (*Gal.* iii), quia nullus omnia implevit, et ita, quilibet spirituali legis opprobrio subjectus fuit.[94]

In the third book, refuting the heretical beliefs of the Jews, Alain had to prove that all those who had died before Christ's birth descended into Hell. Citing several passages from the Old Testament (which, of course, the Jews accepted as authoritative), he concludes: "Nemo ergo in coelum ascendebat, sed omnes qui tunc moriebantur descendebant ad infernum."[95] None could have escaped this fate because of the taint of original sin: "Non est immunis a peccato infans cujus vita est unius diei super terram."[96] For this reason, Christ's sacrifice was necessary: "Mors itaque Christi, peccati originalis apud Patrem hostia et propitiatio fuit."[97] Alain then cites the traditional passages which refer to the Descent, Luke 23:43 and Hosea 13:14. In this book, then, Alain intended to demonstrate to the Jews that Christian doctrine did provide for the salvation of their Fathers.[98]

We have seen that Bernard of Clairvaux, Peter the Lombard, Hugh of St. Victor, and Alain of Lille conservatively associated the Descent with the liberation of Old Testament patriarchs without directly speculating on the fate of the classical pagans. Peter Abelard and Thomas Aquinas, however, ventured to do so.

---

[91] *P.L.,* Vol. 210, col. 343CD.
[92] *P.L.,* Vol. 210, col. 343D.
[93] *P.L.,* Vol. 210, col. 344CD.
[94] *P.L.,* Vol. 210, col. 344CD.
[95] *P.L.,* Vol. 210, cap. xix, col. 418C.
[96] *P.L.,* Vol. 210, cap. xix, col. 418D.
[97] *P.L.,* Vol. 210, col. 419B.
[98] Turner 187.

Both advocates of the value of philosophy, Abelard and Aquinas made strong appeals to the use of reason in understanding the Christian faith. Reason, in Abelard's view, was a necessary adjunct to faith, not a dispensable and separate entity. For example, in his *Dialogus,* a discussion between a Christian, a Jew, and a philosopher, the philosopher rejects the others' religious beliefs because they refuse to give intellectual proofs.[99] This illustrates Abelard's contention in the *Introductio* that we must offer more proof than "Deus id dixerat": "Nec quia Deus id dixerat creditur, sed quia hoc sic esse convincitur, recipitur."[100] Furthermore, reason is the mark by which man is particularly compared to the image of God, and therefore reason is perhaps used most appropriately to investigate God Himself:

> Unde etiam cum per insigne rationis imaginis Dei specialiter homo comparetur, in nihil aliud homo pronius eam figere debuerat, quam in ipsum, cujus imaginem, hoc est expressiorem similitudinem, per hanc obtinebat, et in nullam fortasse rem percipiendam pronior esse credenda est, quam in eam cujus ipsa amplius adepta sit similitudinem.[101]

On the other hand, Abelard does not place reason higher than faith: "Nolo sic esse philosophus, ut recalcitrem Paulo. Non sic esse Aristoteles, ut secludar a Christo."[102] In addition, he recognizes that mere intellectual acceptance is not sufficient for salvation but must be infused with charity:

> Ac nunquam si fidei nostrae primordia statim meritum non habent, ideo ipsa prorsus inutilis est judicanda, quam postmodum charitas subsecuta, obtinet quod illi defuerat.[103]

To refute Gregory the Great's apparent denial of the value of philosophy, Abelard reinterpreted Gregory's statement that faith for which human reason gives proof has no merit ("nec fides habet meritum, cui humana ratio praebet experimentum"). Abelard insists that Gregory means faith gained by reason alone, without divine authority, has no merit, and not that faith and reason are incompatible:

> Qui nec etiam dixit non esse ratiocinandum de fide, nec humana ratione ipsam *discuti vel investigare* debere, *sed non ipsam* apud Deum habere meritum, ad quam non tam divinae auctoritatis inducit testimonium, quam humanae rationis cogit argumentum.[104]

---

[99] *P.L.,* Vol. 178, col. 1615.

[100] *P.L.,* Vol. 178, col. 1050D.

[101] *Introductio,* III. *P.L.,* Vol. 178, col. 1086C.

[102] *Epistola* xvii. *P.L.,* Vol. 178, col. 375C.

[103] *Introductio,* II, 3. *P.L.,* Vol. 178, col. 1051A. Abelard was not unique in this distinction between types of faith. Augustine likewise speaks of his "unformed faith" before baptism in *De Bapt.* III. 16, 21 (*P.L.,* Vol. 43, col. 149). Anselm of Canterbury also makes a distinction between valueless or loveless faith and meritorious faith possessing charity (*Monolog.* 77; *P.L.,* Vol. 158, col. 219C). Aquinas makes the same distinction between *fides informis* and *fides formata* (*In Romanos,* I, lect. 6, VI. 18; also *Summa Theologica* 2-2. 4,4 and 19,5).

[104] *Introductio. P.L.,* Vol. 178, col. 1050CD. The six underlined words are omitted from the

As a final clarification of Abelard's assessment of reason and faith, we know that he believed some gift of divine grace was necessary for a man to study philosophy:

Quantocunque enim tempore in ejus doctrine desudaveris, laborem inaniter consumis, nisi mente tua arcani tanti capacitatem coelestis gratiae munus effecerit. Caeteras vero scientias quibuslibet ingeniis potest exercitii diuturnitas ministrare; haec autem divinae gratiae tantum adscribenda est.[105]

Given the high place accorded to reason in Abelard's writings, it comes as no surprise that he believed that many of the classical philosophers attained Christian truths. As an example, he cites Hermes Trismegistus,[106] identifies the Platonic and Christian Trinities (even claiming that the Platonic World-Soul is the same as the Holy Spirit),[107] and points to the prophecies of Virgil's Fourth Eclogue[108] and the Sibyl.[109]

Abelard seems to attribute the classical achievement of truth to a combination of reason and natural law. He goes so far as to say that the Gospel is nothing more than a reformation of the natural law followed by the philosophers: "Si enim diligentur moralia Evangelii praecepta consideremus, nihil ea aliud quam reformationem legis naturalis inveniemus, quam secutos esse philosophos constat."[110]

Since these philosophers, in Abelard's opinion, could reach an understanding of Christianity, he felt assured of their salvation as well. Two chapters in his *Sic et Non* take up this question of who was delivered from Hell by Christ's descent. First, in *Quod Adam salvatus sit, et contra,* he cites various authorities who affirm that Adam was saved. There are no *contra* arguments on this point.[111] In another chapter, *Quod Christus descendens ad inferos omnes liberavit inde, et contra,* Abelard cites arguments for and against Christ's liberation of all souls in Hell.[112] Although Origen and Ambrose (actually Ambrosiaster) are presented in the affirmative, the majority of authorities cited taught that only those who had anticipated Christ's Incarnation were saved. This seemed to assure the salvation of the Old Testament patriarchs and prophets, but left the position of the classical philosophers vague.

Whereas Augustine had passed over this question, Abelard undertook to prove the salvation of the pagan philosophers. In his *Theologia Christiana,*

P.L. text but supplied by Balliol Ms. CCXCVI, folio 29. Sikes (52) points out that their addition alters the traditional interpretation of this passage and makes Abelard's position more tenable.

[105] *Dialectica.* Taken from Sikes 59, n. 1.
[106] *Introductio,* I, 16, *P.L.,* Vol. 178, cols. 1009–1010.
[107] *Introductio,* I, 18. *P.L.,* Vol. 178, col. 1024B.
[108] *Introductio,* I, 21. *P.L.,* Vol. 178, col. 1031A. *Theol. Christ.* I, 5. *P.L.,* Vol. 178, col. 1163B.
[109] *Introductio,* I, 21. *P.L.,* Vol. 178, col. 1031B. *Theol. Christ.* I, 5. *P.L.,* Vol. 178, col. 1162C.
[110] *Theol. Christ.* II. *P.L.,* Vol. 178, col. 1179D.
[111] *P.L.,* Vol. 178, cap. LVIII, cols. 1427C–1428A.
[112] *P.L.,* Vol. 178, cols. 1468D–1471D.

he asserted that the philosophers' love of virtue had led them to Christian truth:

Quod si id minus videtur esse ad meritum salvationis quod dicitur amore virtutus, et non potius amore Dei, ac si virtutem vel aliquod bonum opus habere possimus, quod non secundum ipsium Deum ac propter ipsum sit: facile est et hoc reperiri apud philosophos, quod summum bonum, quod Deus est, omnium tam principium, id est originem et causam efficientem, quam finem, id est finalem causam constituunt ut omnia, scilicet bona, amore ipsius fiant, cujus ex dono proveniunt.[113]

But while affirming the possibility of salvation of the classical philosophers, Abelard does not directly link it to Christ's descent. In fact, in the *Dialogus* the Christian argues against a literal interpretation of the Descent:

Tum ex Veteri quam ex Novo Testamento innui videtur ea quae de inferno dixerunt, mystice magis quam corporaliter accipi debere, ut videlicet, sicut ille Abrahae sinus, quo suscepta est anima Lazari spiritalis est, non corporalis intelligendus, ita et infernus spiritalis ille cruciatus, quo anima divitis sepulta memoratur.[114]

In addition, Abelard does not link the salvation of the classical philosophers with the salvation of heathen alive after the time of Christ. Under the New Law, baptism and faith are necessary. Thus the soul of Trajan (a pagan Roman emperor of the late first and early second centuries) may have been drawn out of the place of torture, as tradition and legend held. However, his soul was not necessarily received into heaven.[115]

Overall, then, Abelard attempts to prove that reason is an essential complement to faith, although not an adequate substitute for it; however, the use of man's highest reasoning powers—as in philosophy—is necessarily attended by divine grace. Therefore, the classical philosophers had certainly received salvation.

Like Abelard, Aquinas accords reason a prominent position. In fact, his *Summa Theologica* stands as a monument to the role of reason in interpreting the Christian faith. Christianity and philosophy are interwoven almost inextricably: knowledge of the first principles has been implanted in us by God,[116] while the goal of all right thinkers is the contemplation of God ("[O]mnes qui recte senserunt posuerunt finem humanae vitae Dei contemplationem").[117] At the same time, however, there is a clear difference between the theologies of the philosophers and *sacra doctrina*, which "differt secundum genus."[118] Sacred doctrine is not mere knowledge about God but an invitation from God to attain beatitude: "[I]lle qui credit habet

[113] *P.L.*, Vol. 178, col. 1175B.
[114] *P.L.*, Vol. 178, col. 1672C.
[115] *Theol. Christ.* II. *P.L.*, Vol. 178, col. 1204C.
[116] *Contra Gentiles*, I, 7, 2.
[117] *In I. Sent., Prol.*, q. I, a. I.
[118] *Summa Theologica*, 1. 1, 1 ad 2m.

sufficiens inductivem ad credendum; inducitur enim auctoritate divinae doctrinae miraculis confirmatae, et, quod plus est, interiori instinctu Dei invitantis."[119] This invitation does not nullify the value of reason but perfects it. Abelard had earlier responded to Gregory's charge that "fides non habet meritum cui humana ratio praebet experimentum" by changing the interpretation of the statement; Aquinas forthrightly retorts, "fides non destruit rationem, sed excedit eam et perficit."[120]

Aquinas also goes beyond Abelard by making clear that this faith is available to those without the benefit of exposure to Christian teaching, even after the Incarnation. He poses the case of a person reared in the wilderness or among wild animals:

Si enim aliquis taliter nutritus, ductum naturalis rationis sequeretur in appetitu boni et fuga mali, certissime est tenendum quod ei Deus vel per internam inspirationem revelaret ea quae sunt ad credendum necessaria, vel aliquem fidei praedicatorem ad eum dirigeret, sicut misit Petrum ad Cornelium, Act. X.[121]

Thus doing one's best will open the way to whatever is necessary for salvation: "si nos fecerimus quod in nobis est, ut scilicet ductum naturalis rationis sequamur, Deus non deficit nobis ab eo quod nobis est necessarium."[122]

Peter Lombard had used the story of Cornelius primarily to emphasize the necessity of faith; however, Aquinas mentions it to emphasize God's willingness to provide the means to faith. Before the Incarnation, He even provided for the Gentiles several avenues leading to salvation, ranging from implicit faith to direct revelation:

[I]deo sufficiebat eis habere fidem de Redemptore implicite, vel in fide Prophetarum, vel in ipsa divina providentia. Probabile est tamen multis generationibus mysterium redemptionis nostrae ante Christi adventum gentilibus fuisse revelatum, sicut patet ex sybillinis vaticiniis.[123]

As a final proof that at that time explicit faith was not necessary for salvation, Aquinas cites the case of John the Baptist, who doubted Christ's descent into Hell, one of the articles of the Creed:

Joannes Baptista . . . non tamen oportebat quod explicite crederet omnia quae post Christi passionem et resurrectionem tempore gratiae revelata explicite creduntur: non enim suo tempore veritatis cognitio ad suum complementum pervenerat, quod praecipue factum est in adventu Spiritus sancti.[124]

---

[119] *Summa Theologica*, 2-2. 2, 9 ad 3m.

[120] *Quaestiones Disputatae, De Veritate,* Quaestio XIV, *De Fide,* X, ad 9m.

[121] *Quaestiones Disputatae, De Veritate,* XIV, XI, ad 1m.

[122] *Quaestiones Disputatae, De Veritate,* XIV, XI, ad 2m.

[123] *Quaestiones Disputatae, De Veritate,* XIV, XI, ad 5m.

[124] *Quaestiones Disputatae, De Veritate,* XIV, XI, ad 6m. The first authentic mention of the Descent in a Catholic creed comes from Rufinus (d. 395), reporting the activities of his church in Aquileia and pointing out that this formula is found in neither the Roman nor Eastern creed. After Rufinus, though, the formula *descendit ad inferos* appears in many places. (See Quilliet, "Descente," cols. 568–570.) The insertion of this credal formula probably

God even provided sacraments, necessary for salvation, to those alive before Christ's coming. These sacraments pointed to the Saviour's advent:

[S]acramenta necessaria sunt ad humanam salutem. . . . Et ideo oportebat ante Christi adventum esse quaedam signa visibilia quibus homo fidem suam protestaretur de futuro Salvatoris adventu. Et hujusmodi signa dicuntur sacramenta.[125]

Since these sacraments were contained in the Mosaic Law, the Jews of the Old Testament were certainly provided for by God. Therefore, it is not surprising to find Aquinas discussing their liberation from Hell on the occasion of Christ's descent. Their assignment to Hell was based on original sin, nothing else, so that Christ's sacrifice set them free.[126] (After the Descent, baptism sufficed to erase original sin.[127]) Not all were freed from Hell, though. Those without faith in Christ's passion and those with faith but without love were left behind:

Illi autem qui erant in inferno damnatorum, aut penitus fidem passionis Christi non habuerant, sicut infideles; aut si fidem habuerant, nullam conformitatem habebant ad charitatem Christi patientis. Unde nec a peccatis suis erant mundati.[128]

In addition, children without the capacity for faith and free will, and souls undergoing the purification of purgatory, were left behind.[129] However, no virtuous pagans would be left behind, for the truly virtuous would receive God's grace. In fact, if any man did not use his free will to prepare himself for grace, he was guilty of the sin of omission. Thus for Aquinas none in Hell are guilty only of original sin:

[N]on est possibile aliquem adultum esse in solo peccato originali absque gratia; quia statim cum usum liberi arbitrii acceperit, si se ad gratiam praeparaverit, gratiam habebit; alias ipsa negligentia ei imputabitur ad peccatum mortale.[130]

Aquinas also tackled the question of where the virtuous had awaited Christ's descent. Solving Augustine's confusion over whether the bosom of Abraham was in Hell, Aquinas acknowledged the two to be identical. The souls were in the bosom of Abraham to the extent that they were free from punishment, but they were in Hell to the extent that they

---

became irrevocable by the ninth century, when it appeared in the *Ordo romanus* during the time of Pope Nicholas I, 858–867. At that time, the legend revived that the twelve apostles had each brought an article to the creed. This formula was attributed to St. Thomas or St. Philip and thus took on apostolic authority (Quilliet, "Descente," col. 572). See also MacCulloch 67–73.

[125] *Summa Theologica,* 3a. 61,3.
[126] *Summa Theologica,* 3a. 52,5.

Per hoc autem sancti patres detinebantur in inferno, quod eis ad vitam gloriae propter peccatum primi parentis aditus non patebat. Et sic Christus descendens ad inferos, sanctos patres ab inferis liberavit.

[127] *Summa Theologica,* 3a. 52, 5 ad 2m.
[128] *Summa Theologica,* 3a. 52, 6.
[129] *Summa Theologica,* 3a. 52, 7 and 8.
[130] *Quaestiones Disputatae, De Veritate,* XXIV, XII, ad 2m.

desired divine peace.[131] In terms of location, they waited in a limbo which formed a higher part of Hell.[132]

In brief, then, Aquinas holds traditional views on the subject of Christ's descent, but his emphasis on the role of reason and the sufficiency of implicit faith, available to Jews and Gentiles alike before the Incarnation, opens the way to salvation for the classical poets and philosophers.

Aquinas' stand was upheld by Alexander of Hales, who posited the case of a child imprisoned by Saracens. He concludes that if, upon reaching adulthood, the captive did all that he could to live righteously, God would illumine him by secret revelation, either by angel or man. ("Si facit quod in se est Dominus illuminabit eum par occultum inspirationem aut per angelum aut per hominem."[133]) In the same way, man's intelligence can prepare itself to receive an interior voice which will reveal the Christian mysteries: "De incarnatione et redemptione si aptet intellectum suum quantum in se est, vocabitur vocatione interiori, etsi non exteriori."[134] Because of these beliefs, Alexander of Hales contended that a revelation had been granted to the philosophers before Christ. As Job and his friends had been enlightened, so had less-instructed pagans.[135]

The Fourteenth Century

The belief in the harmony of reason and faith, whereby God rewarded the efforts of man's natural intelligence, did not continue into the fourteenth century.[136] In 1277 Étienne Tempier, Bishop of Paris, condemned 219 propositions which veered dangerously near Averroism, or pure rationalism. Gordon Leff sees in this action "a turning-point in the use of Aristotle to support theology, expressing the hostility felt towards associating God and His ways with physical operations in this world."[137]

---

[131] *Summa Theologica,* III (Supp.), LXIX, IV.

[132] *Summa Theologica,* III (Supp.), LXIX, V.

[133] *Summa Theologica,* II, CXIII, m. VIII cas. I. From Janet Coleman, *"Sublimes et Litterati:* The Audience for the Theories of Grace, Justification and Predestination, Traced from the Disputes of the Fourteenth Century *Moderni* to the Vernacular *Piers Plowman,"* Ph.D. diss., Yale University 1970, 142.

[134] *Summa Theologica,* II, CXIII m. VIII cas. I. From Coleman 143.

[135] *Summa Theologica,* III, LXIX a. 3. From Coleman 49.

[136] Étienne Gilson's *Reason and Revelation in the Middle Ages* (New York: Charles Scribner's Sons, 1954) documents the growing opposition between the proponents of faith on the one hand and reason on the other. Paul Vignaux's *Justification et prédestination au XIV° siècle* (Paris: E. Leroux, 1934) also traces this development, primarily by examining the beliefs of four prominent thinkers of the century: Duns Scotus, Pierre d'Auriole, William of Ockham, and Gregory of Rimini. Vignaux concludes that Duns Scotus and Pierre d'Auriole have in common the effort to understand and explain the dealings of God in human salvation, whereas William of Ockham stresses the vanity of such an effort. For Gregory of Rimini, man's understanding is a secondary concern; what matters most is man's absolute incapacity to perform morally good acts by his own unaided will.

[137] Gordon Leff, *Bradwardine and the Pelagians* (Cambridge: Cambridge University Press, 1957) 4. J.A. Robson (*Wyclif and the Oxford Schools* [Cambridge: Cambridge University Press, 1961] 19) succinctly characterizes this period:

In brief, Augustinian neoplatonism was criticised for confounding God and man in a single

Both Duns Scotus and William of Ockham contributed to this split between reason and faith. Duns expanded the list of truths requiring faith
without possibility of proof; Ockham held that natural reason could prove
nothing about God, not even His existence.[138] This stance invalidated such
arguments as Anselm's well-known "ontological proof" of God's
existence[139] and the systematic syntheses of faith and reason developed
by both Augustine and Aquinas.

This divorce of reason and faith was largely due to an exaggerated
emphasis upon the two orders of God's power, His *potentia ordinata* (by
which the world was governed) and *potentia absoluta* (which enjoyed absolute freedom and could override the *potentia ordinata* as God willed). Most
fourteenth-century thinkers split into two opposed extremes on the issue
of *potentia absoluta*, with the controversy primarily centered in the relationship of man's free will and God's all-powerful will.[140] Could a man
rely on unaided free will to help him achieve salvation, or was supernatural
grace necessary to give man any merit in God's eyes? This issue pertains
to the salvation of the virtuous pagans as well, since it seemed that many
of the classical philosophers and poets deserved divine recompense for
their efforts to reach a knowledge of God. In addition, the infinite possibilities open to God's *potentia absoluta* meant that God could grant salvation
as He wished; the pagans were not necessarily damned if they lacked
faith (explicit *or* implicit) in Christ.

William of Ockham, Robert Holcot, Thomas Buckingham, and Adam
of Woodham were among those known as "Pelagians," a name borrowed
from a heresy Augustine had battled centuries before.[141] Ockham and
Holcot accorded to man the power to perform good acts by virtue of his
own will; God's *potentia absoluta* allowed Him the freedom to accept such
acts as worthy of divine sanction. Buckingham and Woodham, however,

---

metaphysical system, for excessive determinism, and for depreciating unduly the play of
divine and human will. Against this the new philosophers placed the transcendence of God
(and the impossibility of knowing him except in so far as his nature was expressed in the
world of being), the primacy of his will, and the radical contingency of all divine and
human acts.

[138] Gilson 85–87.

[139] Anselm, who formulated the famous "credo ut intelligam," proves the existence of
God by assuming a name for Him which makes necessary the statement "God exists." In
the beginning of *Proslogion* 2, Anselm states that God is "aliquid quo nihil cogitari possit."
For a fuller explanation, see Karl Barth's *Anselm: Fides Quaerens Intellectum*, trans. Ian W.
Robertson (London: SCM Press Ltd., 1960).

[140] An overview of this issue is presented in Chapters 1 and 2 of *The Crisis of Will in Piers
Plowman* by John M. Bowers (Washington, D.C.: Catholic University of America Press, 1986).

[141] For a complete treatment of this subject, see J. Ferguson, *Pelagius: A Historical and Theological
Study* (Cambridge: Cambridge University Press, 1956). Briefly, the controversy between
Augustine and Pelagius turned upon the meaning of grace. Augustine emphasized "special
grace" (effected by Christ's crucifixion and mediated through baptism); Pelagius, "general
grace" (God's endowment of human nature which enables us to do His will). Ferguson
(172–175) summarizes: "Thus Augustine lays his stress upon the divine initiative, Pelagius
upon the human response. . . . Augustine won in part because the Church, seeing how God
is greater than man, and the divine initiative greater than the human response, felt that his
emphasis was right."

placed even greater emphasis on God's *potentia absoluta*: God's will alone
determines the value and consequence of man's acts. In effect, this nul-
lified traditional morality, for God's will could transform mortal sin into
a meritorious act. This belief made reason of no avail for salvation. The
Pelagians' chief opponent, Thomas Bradwardine, also denied reason any
spiritual efficacy, but on a different basis: he opposed the Pelagian belief
in man's ability to do good of his own will. For Bradwardine, divine grace
was necessary before man could perform any act of merit.

Before examining these major positions in more detail, we should briefly
consider the opinions of Gregory of Rimini and Richard FitzRalph, note-
worthy for their moderation on this issue. Gregory of Rimini conceded
God's prerogative and ability to deviate from His ordained laws but
contended that this did not make Him unknowable. His *potentia absoluta*
could apply to His creation, but not to His own nature.[142] Richard
FitzRalph basically agreed. Duns had introduced the possibility of God's
potentia absoluta being used to free man from the necessity of grace for
salvation; FitzRalph held that all meritorious actions must be informed
by God's grace and justice.[143] However, he did allow man's free will some
scope in determining its own destiny.[144]

Opposed to the moderate approaches of these two men were, as we
have seen, those who took the concept of *potentia absoluta* to its two opposite
extremes. Ockham was in the forefront of those speculating upon the
consequences of God's *potentia absoluta*. In 1326, 51 articles from his *Sentences*
were condemned at Avignon; the first four invoked God's *potentia absoluta*
as capable of otherwise unthinkable feats:

1. Man can of his own will perform an act worthy of God's grace.
2. God can accept a man without grace into eternal glory and can damn
   a man who has not sinned.
3. Charity is not necessary for divine acceptance.
4. God can remit sin without the sinner first needing grace.[145]

Although these four articles were labeled Pelagian, Ockham disagreed.
His views, he argued, were the opposite: whereas Pelagianism held that
God was bound in justice to reward a good act, Ockham's beliefs set Him
free to act as He would:

Item errorem Pelagius posuit quod si aliquis habet actum bonum ex genere: deus
necessitatur ad conferendum sibi vitam eternam, et non mere ex gratia sua, ita
quod necessario foret iniustus si sibi non tribueret vitam eternam. . . . Ego autem

---

[142] Gordon Leff, *Richard FitzRalph, Commentator of the Sentences* (Manchester: Manchester University Press, 1963) 8.

[143] Leff, *FitzRalph* 158, n. 5. "Perdita iustitia que est instrumentum volendi non potest ipsa
voluntas istam velle nisi per gratiam reddatur" (II, Q 3, 164va).

[144] Leff, *FitzRalph* 16.

[145] Leff, *Bradwardine* 189–192. Also see A. Pelzer, "Les 51 Articles de Guillaume Occam
censurés en Avignon en 1326" in *Revue d'histoire écclesiastique* 18 (1922): 240–271.

pono quod nulla forma nec naturalis nec supernaturalis potest deum sic neces-
sitare.[146]

Robert Holcot agreed that God's *potentia absoluta* allowed Him to dispense
with grace and grant beatitude to natural acts of good:

Dico tunc istam conclusionem: quod deus potest acceptare ad vitam eternam omnes
actus naturales alicuius hominis: et facere omnes actus liberos atque indifferentes
aut non meritorios . . . . dicendo quod actus naturalis sit meritorius si deo placet:
et hoc quia eque libere posset illum acceptare ad vitam eternam.[147]

Furthermore, Holcot contended that God reveals Himself to all who seek
Him: "sed quicumque ad Deum innocenter se habent et rationem natur-
alem exercent studendo . . . Deus eis sufficienter sui communicabit no-
titiam sic quod eis sufficiant salutatem."[148]

Thomas Buckingham and Adam of Woodham carried this even further.
For Buckingham, God's *potentia absoluta* could overturn all order; for example, a man without grace could be saved at the moment of death:

Ad idem arguo sic: non est inconveniens quod aliquis per totam vitam suam fuit
in peccato mortali et sine gratia et nunquam in gratia et tamen in instanti mortis
est sine peccato et salvatus.[149]

In effect, God's will is so powerful in Buckingham's scheme that human
will does not have to strive for good. However, man's will is able of its
own accord to keep him from sin: "Concedo preter tamen charitatem est
una naturalis iustitia qua creatura rationalis potest esse iusta et recta sine
charitate."[150]

For Adam of Woodham, God's *potentia absoluta* exists for the purpose of
overriding His ordained power ("frustra videtur mihi distinguerent doc-
tores de potentia dei ordinata et absoluta nisi aliter posset facere et dis-
ponere de rebus quam disposuit de facto").[151] Therefore, only His will
imposes values of good and bad upon men's actions, and His absolute
will is arbitrary, not bound by any rules: "Respondeo quod rectitudo est
quod vult et rationale est omnino quod fiat sibi."[152] Woodham goes even
beyond Buckingham on this issue. Buckingham felt that sin could be
supplanted by grace at God's will; Woodham asserts that grace and mortal
sin can coexist.[153] As Leff sees it, "The importance of such an attitude
cannot be overstressed: it is to destroy the traditional order by which God

---

[146] Leff, *Bradwardine* 197, n. 2. *Sentences*, Bk. I, dist. 17, q. I I and M.

[147] Leff, *Bradwardine* 217, n. 3. *Sentences*, Bk. I, Q. I, art. 4D.

[148] *Sap. Lect.* 155, MS Balliol Coll. 27 fol. 231 ab-a. From Coleman 150. For a more complete
discussion of Holcot's resolution of the dialectic of God's *potentia absoluta* and *potentia ordinata*,
see H. Oberman, "Facientibus quod in se est Deus non denegat gratium: Robert Holcot OP
and the Beginning of Luther's Theology," *Harvard Theological Review* 55 (1962): 317–342.

[149] Leff, *Bradwardine* 233, n. 1. *Sentences*, Bk. I, dist. 17, q. 6.

[150] Leff, *Bradwardine* 229, n. 2. *Sentences*, q. 6.

[151] Leff, *Bradwardine* 242, n. 1. *Sentences*, Bk. I, dist. 17, q. 3, ms. b.

[152] Leff, *Bradwardine* 243, n. 3. Bk. I, dist. 17, q. 1.

[153] Leff, *Bradwardine* 246. Bk. I, dist. 17, q. 3.

moves and men are moved; it devaluates all hitherto accepted standards of good and evil; and it removes any constant criteria by which anything may be judged."[154]

Like these men, Thomas Bradwardine separated faith and reason, although from the opposite angle. Buckingham and Woodham (and, to a lesser extent, Holcot and Ockham) believed that God was unknowable and that His *potentia absoluta* was unpredictable. But they also allowed man's free will great autonomy, believing that man could use a disposition to do good as a moral claim to grace. (This became known as merit *de congruo*.) Bradwardine agreed that reason could not lead to a knowledge of God. Indeed, the highest truth in philosophy is that we cannot by ourselves know God: "Sapiat ergo sobrie quicunque philosophus et istam veritatem pro maxima Philosophia agnoscat, nihil citra Deum posse cognoscere plene Deum nisi forte per eum."[155] But Bradwardine, far from granting man the possibility of merit *de congruo*, contended that faith alone led to justification in God's eyes: "Sequuntur enim opera iustificatum, non praecedunt iustificandum, sed sola fide sine operibus praecedentibus sit homo iustus."[156] Furthermore, man could not be sure of his status ("Nescit homo utrum amore, an odio dignus sit"),[157] but to follow free will was the path to sin since man could do no good of his own accord:

Nam usus creaturae, si non referatur in Deum, est usus illicitus; ergo peccatum, vel saltem non est recte factum: ergo illa intentio non est recta; nec alicuius intentio sine charitate et gratia gratuito super omnia fertur in Deum.[158]

Thus according to the Pelagians, as Bradwardine branded his opponents, all men could merit grace by using their free will to do good works. Bradwardine, on the other hand, argued that men could do no good without a supernatural infusion of grace, granted by God as He wills, not as man deserves.[159]

A different solution altogether was proposed by Uthred of Boldon, a Benedictine monk in the University of Oxford in the 1360s. Uthred advanced the idea that salvation ultimately depended on a *clara visio* of God at the moment of death. This was granted to all men, not just Christians, so that all are offered the opportunity of accepting or rejecting salvation.[160]

---

[154] Leff, *Bradwardine* 246.

[155] Leff, *Bradwardine* 120, n. 3.

[156] Leff, *Bradwardine* 83, n. 2.

[157] Leff, *Bradwardine* 84, n. 2.

[158] Leff, *Bradwardine* 76, n. 1.

[159] Another extreme determinist was John Wyclif, who paid Bradwardine the compliment of borrowing the term "Pelagians" for those he opposed. Wyclif differed from Bradwardine in emphasizing God's knowledge, not His will, but agreed that no man could perform a meritorious act without the initial act of divine grace working in him (Robson 201, 211). Wyclif's stand eventually led him to a full predestinarianism, whereby a man's acts were totally irrelevant to his damnation (Robson 212).

[160] See M. D. Knowles, "The Censured Opinions of Uthred of Boldon," in *Proceedings of the British Academy* 37 (1951): 305–342. Also, see G. H. Russell, "The Salvation of the Heathen: The Exploration of a Theme in *Piers Plowman*," *Journal of the Warburg and Courtauld Institute* 29 (1966): 101–116, for Uthred's possible influence on *Piers Plowman*, especially in relation to baptism, which becomes irrelevant in Uthred's scheme.

The fourteenth century had a special interest in the subject of pagan salvation due to ongoing dealings with another category of pagans, the Moslems. (Similarly, with the discovery of America two centuries later, the question of the fate of adult infidels would again arise.[161]) R. W. Southern sees the fall of Acre to the Moslems in 1291 as essentially the end of a rational world view of Islam.[162] Up to that time, men such as Raymond Lull (1235–1316) had worked for the conversion of Moslems, viewing them practically as a sect of Christianity with a common philosophical basis. After the fall of Acre, a new attitude favoring their destruction arose for a short time, and the idea of beatitude reserved exclusively for Christians re-appeared in the universities.[163] But this attitude was reversed during the fourteenth century, for missionary efforts took place in the early 1300s. The last recorded Franciscan mission to the East was somewhere in Tartar lands in 1371–74,[164] but in the 1390s many Lollards (including Chaucer's friend Sir Lewis Clifford) joined the Order of the Passion to resist the advance of the Turks. Because of their Lollard bent, they may well have set out intending to convert rather than slay those they hoped to conquer.[165] Thus for most of the fourteenth century, an appreciation of Moslems and a desire to convert them were evident.

This blurring of distinctions between Christianity and Islam, and the renewal of the conversion effort, both indicate the century's interest in the salvation of non-Christians, as well as a concern with foreign cultures. For example, Thomas Hahn, tracing the tradition of the "holy Brahman" in medieval literature, provides the following composite image of these virtuous pagans:

In detail, this western image of the good Indian implies a philosopher, sincere and humble in his search for true wisdom, an ascetic with an air of holiness; moreover, the wise man lives in complete isolation from Christianity, but is devoutly monotheistic, and has attained on his own some understanding of Christianity's universal religious truths, and therefore has some expectation (either explicit or implicit) of salvation.[166]

Hahn discusses at some length the *Alexander B* version of the Alexander legend, written about the middle of the fourteenth century, since it combines the history of the Brahmans and the subject of salvation for non-Christians.[167] He also points to the popularity of *Mandeville's Travels*, with

---

[161] Quilliet, col. 1894. For a study of Muslim influence, see Dorothee Metlitzki's *The Matter of Araby in Medieval England* (New Haven: Yale University Press, 1977).

[162] R. W. Southern, *Western Views of Islam in the Middle Ages* (Cambridge, Mass.: Harvard University Press, 1962) 68.

[163] Coleman 146–147.

[164] Coleman 171.

[165] Coleman 158–159.

[166] Thomas Hahn, "God's Friends: Virtuous Heathen in Later Medieval Thought and English Literature," Ph.D. diss., UCLA 1974, 292. See also Hahn's article "The Indian Tradition in Western Intellectual History," *Viator* 9 (1978): 213–234.

[167] Hahn, "God's Friends" 302–312.

nearly forty surviving English manuscripts, as another evidence of the
fascination of the fourteenth century with the topic of pagan salvation.
In the course of describing a variety of cultures, including the Brahmans,
Mandeville conveys the notion that each person, whether Christian or
pagan, has an inborn knowledge of God's laws and the natural ability to
fulfill them.[168]

As we have seen, this question of the salvation of the virtuous pagan
was of considerable importance from the first through the fourteenth
centuries. With the supposedly apostolic sanction of the concept of
Christ's descent into Hell, the salvation of Adam and the Old Testament
Fathers became almost universally accepted. But from the first and second
centuries, Church leaders were divided on the role of man's reason in
attaining salvation. Those who acknowledged reason as a prerequisite
and/or adjunct to faith tended to look favorably on the salvation of the
classical thinkers they admired. Although these philosophers had not
possessed faith in Christ, it seemed likely that God had made provision
for them in some way. Several possibilities were thus entertained, with
changing emphasis depending on the intellectual climate of the time.

In the early Church, the idea that Christ or His apostles had converted
those in Hell was prominent, perhaps because the early Church itself was
occupied with winning converts. Augustine rejected this view but con-
fessed his inability to determine who had been liberated from Hell. Abelard, making reason almost the equal of revelation, was convinced that
the classical philosophers had been saved. Aquinas added his voice to
others who felt that implicit faith had been sufficient for salvation before
the Incarnation. Although the great masters Augustine and Aquinas had
both viewed reason and faith as compatible, this approach was discredited
in the fourteenth century, which saw proponents of faith and of reason
argue for the exclusivity of one or the other, with only a few voices of
moderation heard. The controversy, which seemed to center on the relative
powers of and relationship between God's will and man's, relates directly
to the question of the salvation of virtuous pagans. If, as the fourteenth-
century "Pelagians" believed, man's free will enabled him to avoid sin
and to do good works, his merit *de congruo* entitled him to God's grace.
This opened salvation to all. In addition, God's *potentia absoluta* could make
anything possible; if even mortal sinners could be saved, surely virtuous
pagans could as well.

The controversies involving religion vs. philosophy, grace vs. works,
God's will vs. man's, were not confined to theological circles but found
their way into secular literature as well. The following chapters will discuss

---

[168] Hahn, "God's Friends" 320–329. Hahn also points out a strain of irony in both *Alexander
B* and *Mandeville's Travels,* for those living without benefit of Christian revelation are often
depicted as leading holier lives than the Christians with whom they are contrasted (312,
319).

two of these works—not primarily to illuminate the theological issues, but rather to demonstrate how an awareness of these issues can yield a deeper understanding of the literature itself. First, however, we will examine both the earliest detailed study of these issues in a vernacular work, Dante's *Divina Commedia,* and the best-known legend of pagan salvation, that of the Emperor Trajan.

III. THE VIRTUOUS PAGAN IN LEGEND AND IN DANTE

While philosophers and theologians speculated on the limitations of reason and the possibility of salvation for virtuous pagans, the issues caught the popular imagination as well. This is evidenced by a few widespread legends of miraculous salvation, proving that the general tendency was toward sympathy for those who had been denied the benefits of revelation or baptism. Since much of the literature presupposes a familiarity with these traditions, it will be helpful to conduct a brief survey of them. In general, these legends fall into three categories: those focusing on baptism, those involving prayers for the dead, and those uniting the pagan past to the Christian present. In addition, Dante's treatment of the issue of pagan salvation is important, for his *Divina Commedia,* a kind of *summa* of medieval Catholicism, is the first vernacular work to make a detailed study of the subject. In this work, Dante both draws upon and expands the traditional legends of virtuous pagans.

Many of the legends involve the question of baptism. Ambrose gave theological justification for the idea of salvation without baptism when he attempted to comfort the sisters of the Emperor Valentinian, who had died as a catechumen without the opportunity of baptism.[1] Perhaps the earliest legend, though, dates from ca. 203 in the story of St. Perpetua, who had a vision of her little brother Dinocrates. He had died of ulcers in the face, and when she first saw him he was suffering from the same affliction. She observed him trying to reach a fountain that was far too high for him. After she prayed for him, she had another vision of him drinking from the fountain, now at his waist-level, and running away in good health and joy. The fountain, of course, signified the baptism which his sister's prayers enabled him to receive.[2]

---

[1] Ambrose was following in the footsteps of other churchmen, such as Bernard, Cyprian, and Augustine, in asserting that baptism could be supplied, in necessity, by faith, hope, and charity. See Louis Capéran, *Le problème du salut des infidèles, essai historique* (Toulouse: Grand Séminaire, 1934) 181.

[2] George Every, *Christian Mythology* (New York: Hamlyn, 1970) 108. Every notes that in St. Augustine's time the story was used as an argument against his doctrine that unbaptized babies must be in Hell. Augustine replied that there was no evidence Dinocrates had not been baptized and that, regardless of baptism, the boy was old enough to distinguish between right and wrong. Thus Augustine allowed for the possibility of a virtuous pagan but saw no innate morality in infants which would justify their salvation, although their suffering might be reduced to a minimum. For a detailed treatment of this topic, see Peter Gumpel, "Unbaptized Infants: May They Be Saved?" *Downside Review* 72 (1964): 342–458.

St. Patrick was credited with two instances of miraculous baptism. In one case, Patrick raised from the dead a pregnant woman and baptized both the mother and the child in her womb.[3] Probably better known was the tale of Patrick's encounter with a giant:

Once, as Patrick was travelling in the plains of the son of Erc, namely in Dichuil and Erchuil, he beheld therein a huge grave, to wit, a hundred and twenty feet in length. The brethren asking *ut suscitaretur*, Patrick then brought to life the dead man who was biding in the grave, and asked tidings of him, namely, when and how he got there, and of what race and of what name he was. He answered Patrick, saying: "I am Cass, son of Glass; and I was the swineherd of Lugar, king of Iruata, and Macc Con's soldiery slew me in the reign of Coirpre Niafer. A hundred years have I been here to-day." Patrick baptized him, and he went again into his grave.[4]

Not all legends emphasized baptism; many involved the question of the efficacy of prayers for the dead. For example, one legend widely accepted in the West relates the story of Falconille, a young girl who after her death appeared to her mother and asked her to pray to St. Thecla. As a result of the saint's intercession, Falconille was received into heaven.[5] Aquinas, in a discussion of whether the souls of the damned can profit by the efforts of the living, quotes a story found in a sermon by John Damascene. The tale recounts how St. Macharius found a skull which identified itself as having belonged to a pagan priest whose soul was now damned in Hell. The saint's prayers rescued the priest from his damnation.[6] Another legend purports that prayer could also suffice for deliverance from Purgatory. Roger of Wendover, the supposed author for the *Chronica* from 1189–1235, tells the story of Roger de Thony, "vir nobilis et miles strenuus," under the date of 1228. When Roger died, his brother asked him in the name of God to speak. The corpse replied by saying that his punishment could be mitigated by the performance of good works, masses, and alms.[7]

Perhaps the most significant legends, though, are those which make a deliberate effort to illustrate the unity of the pagan and Christian worlds. The Scandinavian sagas, for example, often use the theme of the virtuous pagan as a way of reconciling pagan tradition with Church teachings. Lars Lönnroth characterizes this treatment as follows:

... a pagan hero is shown in a situation where he appears to be a sort of precursor, or herald, of Christianity, at the same time retaining enough of the pagan ethics

[3] *The Tripartite Life of Patrick, with Other Documents Relating to That Saint,* ed. and trans. by Whitley Stokes (London, 1887) I, 135. Cited by Paul F. Reichardt, "The Art and Meaning of the Middle English *St. Erkenwald*," Ph.D. diss., Rice University 1971, 20.

[4] *The Tripartite Life of Patrick* 123; cited by Reichardt 30.

[5] Capéran 49–50. Also see J. A. MacCulloch, *The Harrowing of Hell: A Comparative Study of an Early Christian Doctrine* (Edinburgh: T. and T. Clark, 1930) 34.

[6] Henry L. Savage, ed., *St. Erkenwald: A Middle English Poem* (New Haven: Yale University Press, 1926) xx. See *Summa Theologica* III (Supp.), LXXI, IV and V.

[7] Savage xix.

to emphasize the difference between the old and the new religion. It is, however, essential to the theme that the hero should never have been in close contact with the Christian faith—it is primarily his natural nobility, in combination with his good sense, and a half-mystical insight into the workings of nature, that makes him act as if he were already on the verge of conversion.[8]

Lönnroth's statement should remind us of the hero preserved in Anglo-Saxon manuscript, Beowulf, and the ongoing attempt to define the poem and its protagonist as primarily Christian or pagan.[9]

As the sagas attempted to bring together primitive paganism and the new Christian religion, myths were formed to bridge the gap between Christianity and the more civilized paganism of Rome as well. Favorite writers such as Virgil, Cicero, Seneca, Lucan, and Pliny were allegedly converted to Christianity during their lifetimes; from Jerome to Petrarch men thought that letters had been exchanged between Seneca and St. Paul. It was speculated that Cicero, who strongly believed in immortality, had translated the prophecy of the Erythraean Sibyl and announced the coming of the Saviour. Virgil's Fourth Eclogue was read as a prophecy of the Incarnation; some even believed him to be aware of the full import of his words. In the mystery plays, especially those connected with the Nativity, Virgil often appeared with the Sibyl and the Hebrew prophets; "his presence implied that Rome as well as Israel had longed for the new dispensation."[10]

Other pagans anticipated the birth of Christ as well. Bradwardine tells of the opening of a pagan's tomb, in which was found a golden blade beside the corpse. On the blade was written "Christ will be born of the Virgin Mary, and I believe in Him." Christ's birth was also prophesied in a book discovered by King Ferrandus of Castile which told the history of the Jews, the Greeks, and the Romans in three languages. Finally, Bradwardine mentions the case of the three wise men from the East, who correctly understood the appearance of the star of Bethlehem as the sign of Christ's birth.[11]

---

[8] Lars Lönnroth, "Noble Heathen: A Theme in the Sagas," *Scandinavian Studies* 41 (1969): 2.

[9] See, for example, the following articles as representative of this critical debate: Charles Donahue, "*Beowulf*, Ireland, and the Natural Good," *Traditio* 7 (1949–51): 263–278, and "*Beowulf* and Christian Tradition: A Reconsideration from a Celtic Stance," *Traditio* 21 (1965): 55–116; Morton Bloomfield, "Patristics and Old English Literature: Notes on Some Poems," *Comparative Literature* 14 (1962): 36–43 (esp. 39–41); L. D. Benson, "The Pagan Coloring of *Beowulf*," in *Old English Poetry: Fifteen Essays*, ed. Robert P. Creed (Providence, R.I.: Brown University Press, 1967) 193–214; Charles Moorman, "Essential Paganism of Beowulf," *Modern Language Quarterly* 28 (1967): 3–18; K. P. Wintersdorf, "*Beowulf*: The Paganism of Hrothgar's Danes," *Studies in Philology* 78 (1981): 91–119. In addition, several essays in *An Anthology of Beowulf Criticism*, ed. Lewis E. Nicholson (Freeport, N.Y.: Books for Libraries Press, 1963) discuss this issue: F. A. Blackburn, "The Christian Coloring in *Beowulf*," 1–22; Marie Padgett Hamilton, "The Religious Principle in *Beowulf*," 105–136; Margaret E. Goldsmith, "The Christian Perspective in *Beowulf*," 373–386.

[10] Charles T. Davis, *Dante and the Idea of Rome* (Oxford: Clarendon Press, 1957) 14. See, for example, the *First Shepherds' Play* in the Towneley Cycle.

[11] A. J. Minnis, *Chaucer and Pagan Antiquity* (Totowa, N.J.: Rowman and Littlefield, 1982)

A deliberate fusion of Christian and pagan elements is also evident in historical views. For example, in the *Mirabilia,* a compilation of Roman legends and descriptions of the city's monuments, the account of the appearance of the goddess Cybele to Agrippa is followed by the story of the appearance of Mary with her Child to Augustus.[12] In addition, the historian Orosius singled out Rome as guided by God's special providence. He cites a series of examples to prove divine intervention in Roman history, but the most significant is his assertion that when Jesus Christ was born, a spring of oil flowed into the Tiber, signifying the divine anointing of Rome's pagan power.[13] Dante follows Orosius' lead, although he limits his own list of miracles to pagan times. In Chapter V of the fourth book of the *Convivio,* he celebrates the divine origin of Rome, which was "uplifted not by human but by divine citizens, into whom was inspired not human but divine love, in their love of her. And this could not or might not be, save for some special end, purposed by God in so great an infusion of heaven."[14]

It is not surprising, then, that the best-known legend of a virtuous pagan involves Trajan, Roman emperor from A.D. 98 to 117.[15] Because this legend is an analogue for *St. Erkenwald* and in *Piers Plowman* plays a role in the discussion of the requirements for salvation, we will examine the tradition in more detail.[16]

48–49. Gordon Whatley, in "Heathens and Saints: *St. Erkenwald* in Its Legendary Context," *Speculum* 61 (1986): 346–348, discusses the first two of these legends and their analogues in more detail.

[12] Davis 14–15.

[13] Davis 63. Orosius also tells his readers that when Hannibal was at Rome's gates, God sent the hailstorm which defeated him, and that under Claudius a civil war was averted by miraculous intervention.

[14] David Thompson, "Dante's Virtuous Romans," *Dante Studies, with the Annual Report of the Dante Society* 96 (1978): 154. Dante's and Orosius' view of Rome contrasts with that of Augustine, who emphasizes Rome's secular achievement and virtue. As Thompson (155–156) puts it, for Augustine, "God granted them empire to recompense and publicize their deeds, which were accomplished through secular, natural virtues. For Dante, however, the Romans' deeds are not a *cause* of divine favor, but rather *evidence* of 'celestiale infusione' . . . at work in Roman history."

[15] One rare vote of disbelief in this legend comes from Nicholas of Trevisa, who in his translation of Higden's *Poly-Chronicon* 5.7 calls the story of Trajan an idiot's tale: "For so greet riȝtwisnesse it semeþ þat Seint Gregorie wan his soule out of hell. *Trevisa.* So it myȝte seme to a man þat were worse þan wood, and out of riȝt bileve" (Minnis 55).

[16] Much of what follows is indebted to Gaston Paris, *La légende de Trajan* (Paris: Imprimerie Nationale, 1878), perhaps the most comprehensive study of the Trajan legend. Gordon Whatley has recently published another thorough study of the legend which examines it from a different point of view. His article "The Uses of Hagiography: The Legend of Pope Gregory and the Emperor Trajan in the Middle Ages" (*Viator* 15 [1984]: 25–63) traces the development of the Trajan legend through four successive stages: the hagiographical, concentrating primarily on Gregory as representative of the Church's power; the humanistic, in which the emphasis shifts to Trajan's virtues and the legend becomes a kind of "secular hagiography"; the scholastic, in which the legend serves merely as a proof or refutation of various theological arguments; and the "eclectic," in which various fourteenth-century authors conflate the legend with the virtuous pagan issue, usually with an anti-ecclesiastical intent. Thus Whatley sees the legend as evolving full circle from a tale celebrating the efficacy of the Church to one suggesting its worthlessness. He concludes, "The fact that,

The story of Trajan falls into two separate parts, although the first episode serves to justify the second. Historically, Trajan's "justness" grew into a Christian legend based on his letter to Pliny the Younger, governor of Bithynia in Asia Minor around A.D. 112. Pliny had written the emperor concerning the secret society of Christians in his region; Trajan's response, one of moderation and justice, was to avoid a general persecution of the illegal sect.[17] By legend, however, Trajan's name was specially connected with an episode which demonstrated his sense of justice and humility. As he prepared to ride off to battle, a widow approached him and asked for justice for her son, who had been unjustly killed. Trajan, anxious to join the battle, promised that he would satisfy her claim when he returned. "What if you do not return?" the woman insisted. Trajan replied, "My successor will satisfy you." The widow responded, "What will it profit you if another does good?" The emperor descended from his horse, tended to the woman's case, and then rode off to war.[18]

---

by the end of the fourteenth century, it was being asserted that Trajan entered heaven without any help from the said saint [Gregory] reflects, surely, a strong desire to believe that men and women everywhere might please God in their own way without subscribing to the fixed traditions of the Roman Church" (60). Whatley also points out that, properly speaking, Trajan cannot be classified as a virtuous pagan because he lived and died during the Christian era and was cognizant of this new faith. But since Dante and Langland treat Trajan as a virtuous pagan (as Whatley admits), I too have taken the liberty of doing so.

[17] The following is a summary of Trajan's letter given by W. H. C. Frend in *Martyrdom and Persecution in the Early Church* (Garden City, N.Y.: Doubleday and Co., Inc., 1967) 164:

Trajan's reply upheld Pliny's actions including the form of tests applied, and allowed him discretion, albeit within the framework of the Emperor's general policy of restoring strict law and order to the province. There was ... no general edict proscribing Christians, and it was not intended to pronounce one. If Christians, however, were denounced, and proved to be such, they were to be given the chance of repentance and recantation, "that is, by worshipping our gods," and they were not to be sought out (*conquirendi non sunt*). Moreover, anonymous accusations were not to be accepted.

[18] The earliest records of this legend exist in a Latin *vita* of St. Gregory written by a monk of Whitby about A.D. 713. It was followed by *vitae* from Paulus Diaconus about 787 and Johannes Diaconus in the ninth century (Savage xvii–xviii). For the Whitby version, see Bertram Colgrave, ed. and trans., *The Earliest Life of Gregory the Great* (Lawrence, Kan.: University of Kansas Press, 1968); for the text of the two latter versions, see Paris 261–262. For the episode involving Trajan and the widow, I shall rely on the redaction of John of Salisbury's *Policraticus* (1159), which draws on both latter versions and was a popular source for the tale in the Middle Ages (Paul Renucci, *Dante, disciple et juge du monde Gréco-Latin* [Paris: Société d'édition Les Belles Lettres, 1954] 400, n. 778). The *Policraticus* reads as follows:

Quum [Trajanus] jam equum adscendisset ad bellum profecturus, vidua, apprehenso pede illius, miserabiliter lugens sibi justitiam fieri petiit de his qui filium ejus, optimum et innocentissimum juvenem, injuste occiderant. Tu, inquit, Auguste, imperas, et ego tam atrocem injuriam patior?—Ego, ait ille, satisfaciam tibi quum rediero.—Quid, inquit illa, si non redieris?—Successor meus, ait Trajanus, satisfaciet tibi.—Et illa: Quid tibi proderit si alius bene fecerit? Tu mihi debitor es, secundum opera tua mercedem recepturus. Fraus utique est nolle reddere quod debetur. Successor tuus injuriam patientibus pro se tenebitur. Te non liberabit justitia aliena. Bene agetur cum successore tuo si liberavit se ipsum. His verbis motus imperator descendit de equo et causam praesentialiter examinavit et condigna satisfactione viduam consolatus est. (Paris 264)

Paris believes that this tale was probably suggested by a bas relief no longer extant which showed a female figure, symbolizing a province, on her knees before Trajan and his soldiers

The episode is important for several reasons. First, it was employed as a stock example of humility; Dante, for instance, places a sculpture of the scene between Trajan and the widow in the first terrace of Purgatory as an inspiration of humility for those doing penance for their excessive pride (*Purgatorio* X: 74–93).[19] In addition, Trajan's intervention in the affairs of a humble subject serves as a reminder of God's power to intervene; if the hierarchy of medieval society reflected that of heaven, appeals in both realms were not in vain.[20] And, since Trajan revealed himself capable of practicing such virtues of justice, mercy, and humility, it is easy to see why tradition accords him a miraculous salvation.[21] Finally, the episode is important because it places an emphasis upon good works. Each man is accountable for his own actions; leaving justice to another avails nothing.

Trajan's legend underwent some interesting variations as time passed. Probably around the middle of the twelfth century, the legend acquired an additional aspect: on another occasion, the emperor's own son murdered the son of a poor woman. This afforded an opportunity to further embellish Trajan's justice, for he now must punish his own offspring. In a Spanish version, the emperor insists on justice although the woman asks for mercy for the emperor's son; in several German chronicles and the *Mirabilia,* the woman asks for the emperor's son in place of her own; in one French version, the woman loses not only her son but also her only possession, a chicken, and Trajan allows her to choose between his son's death or his substitution for the dead boy. Yet another version, by the German Enenkel, does away with the woman's son altogether and substitutes a daughter, whom Trajan's son dishonors. At the woman's request, the emperor spares his son's life but blinds him. He shares in the punishment, though, so that father and son each lose one eye.[22] In all versions of the legend, the one constant factor is an insistence on the importance of the emperor's just actions, as well as the fact that he accepts responsibility for taking action rather than postponing it or leaving it to another.

---

(292). In addition, the anecdote actually involved Hadrian, as reported by Dion Cassius (Paris 288). (See also Whatley 25–26, n. 2.) Renucci suggests that the anecdote was attributed to Trajan because he was more popular than Hadrian and the person for whom the forum (containing the bas relief) was named. Thus the legend "was born perhaps around the third century from a 'telescoping' of an historical anecdote and a Roman bas-relief" (400, n. 778).

[19] Nancy Vickers examines links between the sculpture of Trajan's column and the sculpture of *Purgatorio* X: the importance of intercession, the existence of a scriptural subtext, an awareness of the power of art but the danger of artistic pride ("Seeing Is Believing: Gregory, Trajan, and Dante's Art," *Dante Studies* 101 [1983]: 67–85.)

[20] Patrick Boyde, *Dante, Philomythes and Philosopher* (Cambridge: Cambridge University Press, 1981) 224.

[21] Aquinas reinforces this with his affirmation in the *De Regimine Principum* that a just prince merits a far higher reward than others. (See Edmund G. Gardner, *Dante's Ten Heavens: A Study of the Paradiso* [London: Archibald Constable and Co. Ltd., 1904] 164.)

[22] Paris 267–276. The *Legenda Aurea* (ed. Th. Graesse [Osnabrück: Otto Zeller, 1965] 196) simply reports:

Fertur quoque, quod cum quidam filius Trajani per urbem equitando nimis lascive discurreret, filium cujusdam viduae interemit, quod cum vidua Trajano lacrimabiliter exponeret, ipse filium suum, qui hoc fecerat, viduae loco filii sui defuncti tradidit et magnifice ipsam dotavit.

The emphasis on works in the first part of the legend is nicely balanced by an emphasis on grace in the second. This portion of the legend tells how Gregory, passing through the forum of Trajan and remembering the emperor's good deeds, wept and prayed for him. Gregory's prayers were heard, and Trajan's pagan soul was released from Hell.[23]

As with the first episode, many variations of the legend appeared. Three are especially persistent: (1) Because Gregory prayed for a damned soul, he had to suffer. In the *Kaiserchronik* of the twelfth century, he agrees to cut short his own life in order to have his prayers answered; in the *Legenda Aurea,* he must choose between constant sickness until his death or two days in purgatory. (2) Many versions tell of the opening of a tomb (often unidentified), revealing Trajan's skull with an intact tongue which asks for the Pope's prayers.[24] (3) In some cases (as in the versions of Aquinas and Guillaume d'Auxerre) Trajan's soul re-enters his body long enough for Gregory to baptize him.[25]

In addition, some dispute arose as to Trajan's ultimate fate. Johannes Diaconus (whose version is presented by the *Chronica Majora* and *Flores Historiarum*) specifies that Trajan did not actually go to Heaven but to Paradise, the region of Hell in which he would be free from pain.[26] Aquinas implies that Trajan is one of many who may have been damned in order to be later recalled to life; on the other hand, Trajan's punishment may not have been dismissed but merely suspended until Judgment Day.[27] Finally, in the *Legenda Aurea,* Jacobus de Voragine concludes his re-telling of the tale by giving a convenient summary of the various speculations on Trajan's fate:

Cujus rei (ut ibidem dicit) testis est oriens omnis et occidens. Super hoc dixerunt quidam, quod Trajanus revocatus fuit ad vitam, ubi gratiam consecutus veniam meruit et sic gloriam obtinuit nec erat in inferno finaliter deputatus nec sententia

---

[23] Paris (278–279) again gives both versions of the episode, by Paulus Diaconus and by Johannes Diaconus.

[24] This variation recalls the story relayed by Aquinas of Macharius' finding of a skull; see p. 37.

[25] Paris 279–285. Aquinas explains that as long as Trajan's soul remained in Hell, he could not be moved to repent or to will good: "Obstinata voluntas nunquam potest flecti nisi in malum. Sed damnati homines erunt obstinati sicut et daemones. Ergo voluntas eorum nunquam poterit esse bona" (*Summa Theologica,* III [Supp.], CI, I).

[26] The passage reads as follows (from *P.L.,* Vol. 75, cols. 105D–106A):

Et notandum quia non legitur Gregorii precibus Trajani anima ab infero liberata, et in paradiso reposita, quod omnino incredibile videtur propter illud quod scriptum est: *Nisi quis renatus fuerit ex aqua et spiritu sancto non intrabit in regnum coelorum (Joann.* iii, 3); sed simpliciter dicitur, ab inferni solummodo cruciatibus liberata. Quod videlicet potest videri credibile quippe cum ita valeat anima in inferno existere, et inferni cruciatus per Dei misericordiam non sentire.

[27] The relevant passage is from *Summa Theologica,* III, (Supp.), LXXIV, V, ad 5:

Vel dicendum, secundum quosdam, quod anima Trajani non fuit simpliciter a reatu poenae aeternae absoluta; sed ejus poena fuit suspensa ad tempus, scilicet usque ad diem judicii. Nec tamen oportet quod hoc fiat communiter per suffragia; quia alia sunt quae lege communi accidunt, et alia quae singulariter ex privilegio aliquibus conceduntur.

definitiva damnatus. Alii dixerunt, quod anima Trajani non fuit simpliciter a reatu poenae aeternae absoluta, sed ejus poena usque ad tempus, scilicet usque ad diem judicii fuit suspensa. Alii, quod poena quo ad locum vel modum aliquem tormenti sub conditione fuit taxata, donec orante Gregorio per Christi gratiam locus vel modus aliquis mutaretur. Alii ut Johannes dyaconus, qui hanc legendam compilavit, quod non legitur orasse, sed flevisse; et frequenter dominus misertus concedit, quod homo quamvis desiderans petere non praesumit, et quod ejus anima non est ab inferno liberata et in paradiso reposita, sed simpliciter ab inferni cruciatibus liberata. Valet enim (ut dicit) anima et in inferno existere et inferni cruciatus per Dei misericordiam non sentire. Alii, quod poena aeterna consistit in duobus, scilicet in poena sensus et in poena damni, quod est carentia visionis divinae. Poena igitur aeterna quantum ad primum est sibi dimissa, sed quantum ad secundum retenta.[28]

As is evident from even this brief summary, the story of Trajan's salvation raised some of the same questions the fourteenth-century theologians were wrestling with: Can a man be saved by his own works? (Although Gregory must act as intercessor, the story does have a basic element of Pelagianism in its implicit assumption that Trajan *deserves* salvation.) Is baptism necessary for salvation? Can a pagan actually be received into heaven, or must he accept a lesser reward? We find these questions taken up again in Dante's great work, the *Divina Commedia*. The fate of the virtuous pagan is one of the few themes to appear in all three books.[29]

Reading the *Inferno* alone, one could conclude that Dante denied salvation to all pagans. Even Virgil, whom Christian tradition regarded as a prophet of Christ's birth, is consigned to Limbo. Dante, like Aquinas, envisions a "Limbo" in which suffering is reduced to a minimum. Aquinas designates Limbo as the habitation of unbaptized children and (before the Harrowing) the Old Testament Fathers; Dante places in Limbo unbaptized children (glossed over with the one word "infanti" in *Inferno* IV. 30) and adult pagans. (*Inferno* IV. 55–61 confirms that the Fathers also resided in Dante's Limbo until the Harrowing.[30]) We can see, then, a basic disagreement between Aquinas and Dante:

... both Dante and Aquinas think that the infidels *failed* to attain the light of Revelation. Aquinas, however, sees in this failure a personal sin of omission to be added to original sin, and thus must exclude pagans from Limbo. Dante, on

---

[28] *Legenda Aurea*, ed. Graesse, 197.

[29] Gino Rizzo, "Dante and the Virtuous Pagans," in *A Dante Symposium. In Commemoration of the 700th Anniversary of the Poet's Birth (1265–1965)*, ed. William DeSua and Gino Rizzo, University of North Carolina Studies in the Romance Languages and Literatures 58 (Chapel Hill, N.C.: University of North Carolina Press, 1965) 139, points out that the gradual unfolding of the issue of the virtuous pagan matches the pilgrim's own enlightenment. "The theme of the virtuous pagan represents therefore an essential element of Dante's *itinerarium mentis in Deum*, giving substance and structure both to his spiritual experience and to the pattern of his vision." In an earlier study, Yvonne Batard (*Dante, Minerve, et Apollon* [Paris: Société d'édition Les Belles Lettres, 1952] 195-222) also sees the issue of the virtuous pagan as a "privileged theme" which evolves throughout the poem.

[30] References to the *Divine Comedy* are from John D. Sinclair's translation (1939; New York: Oxford University Press, 1981).

the other hand, represents this failure as the inability of human nature to attain Revelation without the help of divine grace, and thus confines his pagans to Limbo.[31]

Not *all* pagans are in Limbo, however; a high proportion of the souls actually named in the remaining levels of the Inferno (32 out of 116) are pagans.[32] Later, in the *Purgatorio* (VII. 35–36), Virgil explains to Sordello that the adults in Limbo did practice all the natural virtues; obviously those in torment did not.

Virgil himself remains the most puzzling case in the *Inferno.* Dante presents him sympathetically; his Fourth Eclogue (as interpreted in the Middle Ages) would seem to prove his implicit faith in a Redeemer; in *Purgatorio* XXII Statius reveals that Virgil's writings led him to an acceptance of Christianity.[33] Yet despite all this, we learn as early as the second canto that Virgil resides in Limbo.[34]

We leave the *Inferno,* then, with no indication that pagan salvation is possible. Even Plato and Socrates, who were perhaps closest in their beliefs to Christianity, are specifically mentioned as inhabitants of Limbo (*Inferno* IV. 134). This conservative depiction of Limbo does serve at least two purposes, though. Theologically, it illustrates the chasm between the very pinnacle of human reason and Christian revelation.[35] And, artistically, Dante may have used his acceptance by the greatest poets of Limbo to mark his own worth as surpassing theirs because it was dedicated to the service of God (as Augustine recognized the worth of the pagans but condemned them because their works were directed to personal fame, not to God's glory).

With the fate of the *Inferno* pagans in mind, then, we are surprised to find Cato as the guardian of the shores of Purgatory. Not only a pagan but also a suicide, his presence in Purgatory indicates an eventual salvation.[36] Cato's situation has tantalized commentators of the *Purgatorio,* but no definitive answer for his selection has been found.[37]

---

[31] Rizzo 19. Batard sees in this mixture of unbaptized infants and adult pagans an element of hope. Their condition, described as "sospesi," she interprets as "uncertain," meaning not yet fixed (200).

[32] Kenelm Foster, *The Two Dantes and Other Studies* (London: Darton, Longman and Todd, 1977) 187.

[33] Statius likens Virgil to a man who carries a light behind him to illumine the way for them, with no benefit to himself (*Purgatorio* XXII. 67–73). This image makes clear the function of the light of Limbo enclosed in darkness, "un foco ch'emisperio di tenebre vincìa" (*Inferno* IV. 68–69); see Rizzo 132.

[34] *Inferno* II. 52, "Io era tra color che son sospesi." Batard argues for Virgil's eventual salvation (200–201); otherwise, she asks, why would Beatrice promise to commend him to God, and why would he feel shame when Cato reproves the souls who tarry on the shores of Purgatory to enjoy Casella's song?

[35] Rizzo 130.

[36] Virgil also indicates as much when he refers to Cato's vesture which will be so bright one day: "la vesta ch'al gran dì sarà sì chiara" (*Purgatorio* I. 75). Also, Cato indicates in ll. 89–90 that he was delivered from Hell during the Harrowing.

[37] Two persuasive interpretations are Renucci's claim (307–308) that as Cato died for liberty, it is appropriate to find him on the shore of liberty, and Rizzo's explanation (124)

Important for our purposes, though, is the fact that the appearance of Cato offers an alternative fate for pagans. This theme is subtly highlighted as the travelers progress through the terraces of Purgatory, on which classical and Biblical representations are paired. Indeed, one critic has noted that "there are more connections made between the laws of the pagans and of the Christians than between the Old Testament and New Testament."[38]

The apparent salvation of Cato, plus the linking of pagan and Christian in the art of the terrace walls, prepares us for the final presentation of the virtuous pagan theme in the *Paradiso*. In Canto XVIII, Dante ascends into the sphere of Jupiter, mythological ruler of the gods, and watches as a multitude of souls—rulers themselves while on earth—spell out the words "diligite iustitiam qui iudicatis terram" (XVIII. 91–93) and then proclaim with one voice, "For being just and merciful I am here exalted" (Per esser giusto e pio / son io qui essaltato" [XIX. 13–14]). The final "M" of the formation then transforms itself into an eagle, symbol of the Roman Empire. The words formed and spoken by the blessed souls, their common voice, and the eagle symbol point unmistakably to two linked concepts: justice and unity. In a realm which apprehends Divine Justice without a veil ("che 'l vostro non l'apprende con velami" [XIX.30]), and reminded of the unity of all mankind, Dante appropriately turns to a long-held question, the fate of pagans. Does divine justice condemn a man born on the banks of the Indus who has never heard of Christ (XIX. 30–78)?[39]

The question itself is set between two assertions, one negative and one positive, about God's accessibility to the human mind. In XIX. 40–63, the souls sing of God's transcendence: we can penetrate the workings of Eternal Justice in the same way that our eyes can penetrate the sea—the bottom of the sea exists, but its great depth prevents us from seeing it. From the shore we can see the bottom, but it is a false perception of the water's depth (XIX. 58–63). Therefore the pilgrim is presumptuous in questioning God's justice, for he is in no position to gauge the depth of that justice. At the same time, however, the spirits declare that all the goodness known to man radiates from the Supreme Good (XIX. 86–90), and thus man *can* understand God, but only to a limited degree.[40]

---

that Dante, in the *Convivio* (IV, v, vi, xxvii) and *De Monarchia* (II, v) saw in Cato's death "a sacrifice made on the altar of his political commitment and moral freedom." Even Augustine and Aquinas sanctioned suicide "when inspired by a divine instinct to show forth an example of fortitude." In addition, in *Convivio* IV, xxviii, Dante found Cato worthy of signifying God.

[38] Renucci 117.

[39] We have seen that Aquinas and Alexander of Hales posed similar questions; see pp. 26, 28. Whatley points out that Dante is here alluding to the Western tradition of the holiness of the Indian Brahmans and their probable salvation (40, n. 58). He refers us to two articles on this subject by Thomas Hahn: "The Indian Tradition in Western Intellectual History," *Viator* 9 (1978): 213–234; and "I 'gentili' e 'un uom nasce a la riva / de l'Indo,' " *L'Alighieri* 18.2 (1977): 3–8.

[40] Foster concludes, "In fine, Dante is saying, *not* that God's ways are wholly beyond our discerning, but rather that our discernment of them is extremely limited, although real as far as it goes" (146).

All of this, of course, does not directly answer Dante's question; however, it does caution him (and us) that he may not fully understand the answer he receives, which is as follows: "To this kingdom none ever rose who did not believe in Christ, either before or after He was nailed to the tree" ("A questo regno / non salì mai chi non credette 'n Cristo, / vel pria vel poi ch'el si chiavasse al legno" [XIX. 103–105]). This orthodox maxim is not in itself surprising, but its application mystifies Dante when he realizes that two "pagans" are among the stars forming the eagle's eye and eyebrow. Furthermore, they span the centuries, so that they illustrate both points of the maxim, belief in Christ both before and after the Crucifixion.

Dante's choice of virtuous pagans is interesting. He follows tradition by specifying one of them as Trajan; in accordance with one version of the legend, the spirits tell Dante that Trajan returned to the flesh long enough to become a Christian (XX. 112–117).[41] More surprising is Dante's choice of Ripheus, a victim of the Trojan War described briefly in the Aeneid: "Ripheus, too, falls, foremost in justice among the Trojans, and most zealous for the right" ("Cadit et Ripheus, iustissimus unus / Qui fuit in Teucris, et servantissimus aequi").[42]

Dante has thus wisely chosen the two virtuous pagans in the Paradiso. One's salvation was almost universally accepted by tradition; the other was so obscure that no one could raise objections.[43] In addition, both were renowned for their extraordinary justness and, according to the souls in Jupiter's sphere, possessed an explicit faith in Christ. Thanks to Gregory's intercession, Trajan was reanimated so that his will could be moved, while God revealed to Ripheus the coming Messiah: "The other [Ripheus] . . . set all his love below on righteousness; therefore from grace to grace God opened his eyes to our coming redemption" ("L'altra . . . tutto suo amor là giù pose a drittura; / per che, di grazia in grazia, Dio li aperse / l'occhio alla nostra redenzion futura" [XX. 118, 121–123]). The fact that both

---

[41] A.C. Charity (Events and Their Afterlife: The Dialectics of Christian Typology in the Bible and Dante [Cambridge: Cambridge University Press, 1966] 230, 248) also points out that conversion is, above all, the following of Christ, and that Trajan's salvation is a foreshadowing of Dante's own. Following in Christ's footsteps, both Trajan and Dante descend into Hell but then journey to the heavenly spheres. Thus Charity sees Trajan as a "type" of Dante and their experiences as typological repetitions of Christ's. Pursuing a different line of argument, both Whatley (47) and Batard (195–222) see in Trajan's salvation real hope for the eventual salvation of all the souls in Limbo.

[42] From Aeneid II, 426–427. English translation by C. H. Grandgent, ed., La Divina Commedia by Dante Alighieri, rev. Charles S. Singleton (Cambridge, Mass.: Harvard University Press, 1972) 802. Grandgent observes that "Nowhere, before Dante, do we find any suggestion that this Trojan prince attained Heaven, nor that he was of particular importance." We should note, however, that both Ripheus (as a Trojan and therefore an ancestor of the Romans) and Trajan (as a Roman emperor) represent for Dante the virtuous men of early Rome who brought the Empire divine favor. It also seems especially fitting that Ripheus, although born centuries before Christ, should be linked to the city which serves as the seat of the Church. (Additional references to Ripheus are in Aeneid II, 339 and 394.)

[43] T. P. Dunning, "Langland and the Salvation of the Heathen," Medium Aevum 12 (1943): 54.

Trajan and Ripheus apparently had an explicit belief in Christ may explain why so many pagans have been left behind in Limbo, despite the fact that medieval theology allowed for salvation by implicit faith as well.[44]

Another characteristic shared by Trajan and Ripheus is their devotion to the Roman Empire.[45] Placed next to each other, these two souls oppose the soul of Constantine in the formation of the eagle's eye. Trajan had expanded the Empire's boundaries to the Persian Gulf but had preserved Rome as the capital city; Ripheus had fought the Greeks and died in the battle to repel them. In contrast, Constantine had given in to the enemy by moving the capital from Rome to Byzantium, diminishing the heritage of the Caesars. Thus, although Dante is obliged to place Constantine in heaven (Constantine did, after all, institute Christianity as the official religion of the Empire), he symbolically places him at the extreme eastern ("Oriental") point of the eagle's eye, opposite two of the Empire's champions.[46]

Dante's choice of Ripheus also serves as the last stage of a gradual enlightenment on the question of baptism. In Limbo, Virgil had explained that the souls there had not sinned but lacked baptism ("ch'ei non peccaro; e s'elli hanno mercedi / non basta, perchè non ebber battesmo / ch'è porta della fede che tu credi" [*Inferno* IV. 34–36]). The simple explanation suits Dante's limited understanding at the outset of his journey. In the *Purgatorio,* however, Virgil modifies his former explanation and states that he abides "with those who were not clothed with the three holy virtues but without sin knew the others and followed them every one" ("con quei che le tre sante / virtù non si vestiro, et sanza vizio / connober l'altre e seguir tutte quante" [*Purgatorio* VII. 34–36]). The issue of baptism seems here to be omitted entirely. The salvation of Ripheus, however, ties these two passages together, for in *Paradiso* XX, we learn that Ripheus was baptized by the three maidens—Faith, Hope, and Charity—that Dante had seen standing by the right wheel of the chariot in the Earthly Paradise (*Purgatorio* XXIX. 121–129). These allegorical figures "stood for

---

[44] Both Rizzo (136) and Foster (185–186) point out Dante's emphasis on explicit faith. Foster observes that, at least in these two cases, this required the working of miracles, so that the method of salvation for pagans is extremely exceptional. In addition, he notes that the pagans' lack of saving faith is represented not as a moral defect but as an intellectual one.

[45] Indeed, Gardner believes that "Dante's main objective . . . is clearly to indicate that the men whom he regards as the ancestors of the Roman People were not without divine light" (168).

[46] A. Pézard, "Riphée ou la naissance d'un mythe," *Revue des Études Italiennes* 25 (1979): 18. Renucci (321) agrees with this symbolic alignment of Trajan and Ripheus diametrically opposed to Constantine. Pézard discounts two patterns of the eagle's eye proposed by other critics and explains his rationale for conceiving of the eye as a perfect circle around which the souls are located at regular intervals. Thus he sees Ripheus and Trajan on the upward curve leading to Hezekiah at the highest point; Constantine and William are found on the declining curve of the circle (9–22). We should also remember that for Dante, many of the evils of the Church derived from the "donation of Constantine," whereby the Church received its first secular endowment. (Constantine gave the Lateran in Rome to the Papacy in gratitude for recovering from a dire illness.)

baptism to him more than a thousand years before baptizing" ("Quelle
tre donne li fur per battesmo / che tu vedesti dalla destra rota, / dinanzi
al battezzar piu d'un millesmo" [*Paradiso* XX. 127–129]). Thus literal baptism is not necessary, but a figurative baptism by the three theological
virtues is an absolute prerequisite for salvation. This gradual unfolding
of the meaning of baptism is paralleled by the progression of the pilgrim
himself; Dante progresses from natural understanding to divine revelation
when he crosses the river and is presented to Beatrice by the three theological virtues. This symbolizes his own "baptism" by Faith, Hope, and
Charity.[47] Dante's view of baptism is not eccentric; Aquinas and Augustine
had also sanctioned the idea of salvation without literal baptism.[48]

In summary, we can see that for Dante the issue of salvation for pagans
was a significant concern. Dante follows Aquinas in his understanding
of baptism, but he is surprisingly conservative in his estimation of the
means of grace for pagans. Setting aside the doctrine of implicit faith, he
seems to insist on explicit faith for salvation, which (at least in the cases
of Trajan and Ripheus) required miraculous divine intervention. At the
same time, however, Canto XX of the *Paradiso* stresses the ultimate un-
knowability of the ways of God; man cannot presume to fathom His
judgments. Perhaps for this reason the salvation of Cato remains inex-
plicable; he seems to fall into a different category altogether from the
pagans of the *Paradiso*.

Dante, of course, was not alone in his concerns. Besides the surviving
legends and traditions already mentioned, other evidence exists of a growing tolerance for the idea of pagan salvation.[49] M.E. Thomas notes that a

---

[47] See Charles Singleton, *Journey to Beatrice*, Vol. II of *Dante Studies* (Cambridge, Mass.: Harvard University Press, 1954).

[48] For Aquinas' views, see *Summa Theologica* 3. 66, 11; 68, 2. Augustine's opinion can be found in *De Baptis. contr. donat.*, IV, XXII. There still existed, of course, an opposing viewpoint which contended that the sacrament of baptism was literally mandatory for salvation, based on the text of Mark 16:16: "He that believeth and is baptized shall be saved." Augustine himself held this rigorous view in the case of infants who, without baptism, were consigned to Limbo. (See *De Civitate Dei* XIII, XIV; *Enchiridion* XCIII; *De Genesi ad litteram* X, XI, XIX; *Contra Julianum* III, CXCIX.) Cyprian (*Ep.* LXIV) was another standard authority on this point.

[49] We should note, however, that for one group of non-Christians, the Jews, little tolerance existed at any time in England during the Middle Ages. Esther Panitz reports that "Among simple Christian folk it was commonplace to assume that Jews poisoned wells, helped spread the Black Death, desecrated the Host, and slaughtered Christian children for arcane religious purposes" (*The Alien in Their Midst* [East Brunswick, N.J.: Associated University Presses, Inc., 1981] 25). The Jews were accused of ritual murders, first of William of Norwich in 1144 (Edward Calisch, *The Jew in English Literature* [1909; Port Washington, N.Y.: Kennikat Press, Inc., 1969] 38), with other accusations following in 1181, 1192, and 1234. Then in 1255 came the most sensational of all, the death of the boy-martyr Hugh of Lincoln (Montagu F. Modder, *The Jew in the Literature of England* [1939; New York: Meridian Books, Inc., 1960] 11). Massacres of Jews occurred in 1189 and at the coronation of Richard II (Calisch 20), and decrees were passed in 1222 and 1275 compelling Jews to wear badges on their breasts (Modder 7). Finally, on July 18, 1290, the Jews were ordered to leave England by All Saints' Day of that year; nominally and legally there were no Jews in England until Cromwell's time, 365 years later (Calisch 41). This animosity, however, was directed only toward "modern" Jews; those who had lived before the time of the Incarnation were regarded with respect and reverence, as evidenced in the mystery plays (Calisch 19).

"humanitarian" view of salvation which would include all virtuous souls (both Christian and pagan) spread across a wide spectrum of society in the fourteenth century, from mystics such as Rulman Merswin of Strassburg and Julian of Norwich to the orthodox churchman Sacchetti to the cynical author of *Mandeville's Travels.*[50] As the following chapters will prove, at least two authors of secular Middle English literature were also intrigued by the idea of salvation for the virtuous pagan, especially in connection with Christ's Harrowing of Hell. The *Erkenwald*-poet makes the issue of the virtuous pagan the central focus of his tale, while William Langland uses it as a prominent theme of *Piers Plowman.*

---

[50] M.E. Thomas, *Medieval Skepticism and Chaucer* (New York: William-Frederick Press, 1950) 67. As Thomas sees a "humanitarianism" in the acceptance of salvation for virtuous pagans, so Foster sees the theme as an indication of humanism in Dante, representing "a point of transition between the scholastic culture which so largely formed Dante and the humanist culture which followed it and which Dante in some ways . . . prepared and foreshadowed" ("Religion and Philosophy in Dante," in *The Mind of Dante,* ed. U. Limentani [Cambridge: Cambridge University Press, 1965] 54).

IV. ST. ERKENWALD'S HARROWING OF HELL

Although *St. Erkenwald* has been hailed as "much the best saint's legend in Middle English,"[1] some question exists as to its actual genre.[2] This is not the typical saint's life of loosely connected

---

[1] T. McAlindon, "Hagiography into Art: A Study of *St. Erkenwald,*" *Studies in Philology* 67 (1970): 472. Mary-Ann Stouck, in "'Mournynge and Myrthe' in the Alliterative *St. Erkenwald,*" *Chaucer Review* 10 (1976): 243–254, analyzes in more detail precisely how the *Erkenwald*-poet improves upon the traditional saint's legend. Tim Lally ("The Gothic Aesthetic of the Middle English *St. Erkenwald,*" *Ball State University Forum* 20/3 [1979]: 2–10) adds to our appreciation of the poem by examining the principal Gothic tenet of discontinuity held in unity, here expressed "in a rich complexity of narrative structure, moral attitude, imagery, and affective pattern" (2).

[2] The questions of authorship and source have also been primary. Larry Benson gives his arguments against, as well as a summary of the case for, the *Pearl*-poet's authorship of the poem in his article "The Authorship of *St. Erkenwald,*" *Journal of English and Germanic Philology* 64 (1965): 393–405. More recently, Clifford Peterson (ed., *Saint Erkenwald* [Philadelphia: University of Pennsylvania Press, 1977] 20–23) has advanced John Massey of Cotton as the author of *St. Erkenwald* and *Sir Gawain and the Green Knight,* and perhaps the other Cotton Nero poems as well.
The question of source is equally complicated. Many analogues of the work exist, but none is an exact counterpart. For example, St. Macharius was reputed to have discovered the head of a pagan priest who was delivered from Hell by prayer (see p. 37). This story, however, lacks the detail of the miraculously preserved body and its mysterious identity. In another analogue, St. Patrick was credited with restoring to life and baptizing a swineherd (see p. 37). But these figures lack the majesty of the pagan judge in *Erkenwald,* and an actual deliverance from torment is not implied. Instead, they seem to have waited dormantly for St. Patrick's arrival. Henry Savage, editor of *St. Erkenwald: A Middle English Poem* (New Haven: Yale University Press, 1926), points out that the *Chronica Majora* reports several discoveries of undecayed bodies, both Christian and (in the case of Pallas, from the *Aeneid*) pagan (xxii–xxiii). Again, however, the analogues are not exact. Peterson (36–37, 39) mentions Erkenwald's reputation as the founder of St. Paul's and a number of features shared by *St. Erkenwald* and Jacopo della Lana's commentary on Dante, written in the early fourteenth century. Perhaps the closest analogue—certainly the best known one in the Middle Ages—is the story of Trajan and Pope Gregory which was examined in the previous chapter. The tale is recounted or mentioned in several medieval works. (See, for example, the *Chronica Majora, Flores Historiarum, Speculum Historiale, Policraticus, Polychronicon,* and *Summa Praedicantium.* Savage [xvii, n. 9] offers a more complete list.) Gordon Whatley, in "Heathens and Saints: *St. Erkenwald* in Its Legendary Context," *Speculum* 61 (1986): 330–363, argues strongly that the poem is a skillful synthesis of the Gregory/Trajan legend and the Latin *vitae, miracula,* and liturgical offices of the saint. (See also his articles "The Middle English *St. Erkenwald* and Its Liturgical Context," *Mediaevalia* 8 [1982]: 277–306, and "*Vita Erkenwaldi:* An Anglo-Norman's Life of an Anglo-Saxon Saint," *Manuscripta* 27 [1983]: 67–81.) Like Whatley, Sandra Cairns, in "Fact and Fiction in the Middle English *De Erkenwaldo,*" *Neuphilologische Mitteilungen* 83 (1982): 430–438, also analyzes the associations between the historical/legendary details of Erkenwald's life and the poem in the Cotton Nero manuscript. Both Whatley and Cairns discuss the legendary dispute, after Erkenwald's death, over the proper burial location for the saint's body, but come to opposite conclusions. Cairns perceives that the omission of this well-known feature of the *vita,* along with the omission of other commonly known details, is a contribution to the poem's theme: Like the clerks in the poem, the audience should not waste its time trying to find documentary evidence for the story but should

episodes but a tightly constructed narrative in which a pagan, not a saint, receives primary emphasis. One reader justifies this work as a saint's life by establishing two modes of hagiographic writing: the episodic structure of an entire life and the cultivation of a single episode. These forms are further distinguished by a difference in purpose:

In the saint's life, the aim is to portray a model of Christian virtue and human perfection which may be imitated; the method is to accumulate exemplary incidents and actions. The hagiographic tale, on the other hand, is designed to present a single action or event in the life of a saint, and its aim is to extract a particular moral lesson from this one event.[3]

Clearly, *St. Erkenwald* fits under the rubric of hagiographic tale, which necessitates a definition of the moral lesson it conveys. That lesson, the theme of the poem, is a subject of critical disagreement.

Three primary interpretations of the poem's message exist. Larry Benson, pointing out the unusual periphrases for God as Judge of man, sees

---

acknowledge the truth of its message (437). Whatley, however, points out that the same "troubulle in þe pepul / And such a cry aboute a cors" (ll. 109–110) occur in both the *Vita Erkenwaldi* and *St. Erkenwald,* with a "uir religiosus" in both cases calming the crowd and reminding them to seek divine aid. In the *Vita,* the waters of the River Hyde divide, making it clear that God wishes Erkenwald's relics laid to rest in London. This miracle, like the parting of the Red Sea, can be read as a figure of baptism, the sacrament most prominent in *St. Erkenwald* ("Heathens" 356–358).

Along with the framework of the Trajan legend and the Erkenwald liturgy and *vitae,* two other threads probably contributed to the writing of *St. Erkenwald.* One is the Belgian legend of Erkenbald, first recounted in the *Dialogus Miraculorum* of Caesarius of Heisterbach about 1222 and later in the *Alphabetum Narrationum* and the *Dialogus,* collections of medieval exempla. According to the tale, Erkenbald, "vir nobilis et potens, erat tantus amator iustitiae, ut nullam in iudiciis respeceret personam." He lived up to his reputation on his deathbed by killing his nephew, who had attacked a maiden of the household. When the priest consequently refused to give him the Last Sacrament, Erkenbald showed him the Host already on his tongue as a sign of God's approval of his justness. (See Laura A. Hibbard, "Erkenbald the Belgian: A Study in Medieval Exempla of Justice," *Modern Philology* 17 [1920]: 670–671.) The similarity of name and the association with extraordinary justness may help explain why the pagan judge's fate depended on St. Erkenwald rather than another holy man.

The other factor which probably contributed to the work was the discovery of either a corpse or a head in St. Paul's, which we know was built on the site of an ancient Roman cemetery (Hibbard 137). This event was mentioned by Friar Nicholas Philip, OFM, in a sermon dated 1431; concluding an exemplum on chastity, Friar Philip writes, "Pro quo nota historiam de homine mortuo reperto integro in ecclesia sancti Pauli post diem sepelicionis sue per annos multos" (Siegfried Wenzel, "St. Erkenwald and the Uncorrupted Body," *Notes and Queries* 226 [Feb., 1981]: 13). A casual reference to the event was also made by John de Bromyard in the *Summa Praedicantium:* "Nota de iudice cuius caput Londoniis in fundamentum ecclesiae Sancti Pauli inventum fuit" (Hibbard 136).

Finally, we know that in 1386 Robert de Braybroke, Bishop of London, issued a pastoral letter establishing the two commemorative feast-days of St. Erkenwald as feast-days of the first class. Thus Savage suggests this date for the poem, since popular devotion to St. Erkenwald was at its peak (lxxv–lxxvi). Hibbard agrees, noting that "It was in this century and it was in this period that a monastic writer would have seized most willingly on any suggestion for a new miracle tale concerning Erkenwald (136; for further information, Hibbard directs us to Sir William Dugdale, *History of St. Paul's Cathedral* [London: T. Warren, 1658]). On the other hand, Peterson (12–15) argues that the poem was probably written between 1380 and 1420, but "later in that period rather than earlier" (15).

[3]Paul F. Reichardt, "The Art and Meaning of the Middle English *St. Erkenwald,*" Ph.D. diss., Rice University 1971, 17.

the major theme as God's justice.[4] In a related vein, Lester Faigley reads
the poem typologically, seeing in the pagan a judge under the "Old Law"
of strict justice, contrasted with St. Erkenwald as a judge under the "New
Law" of mercy.[5] Vincent Petronella, however, points to transformation as
the poem's main theme: the church, the pagan judge, the rowdy people
are transformed through the miracle.[6] And finally, Arnold Davidson, T.
McAlindon, Paul Reichardt, Sandra Cairns, and Gordon Whatley argue
for the poem's contrast between the limitations of human reason and the
miraculous power of God, with Whatley emphasizing the importance of
Erkenwald's ecclesiastical role.[7]

As Reichardt and Russell Peck indicate, the contrast between human
and divine power is shown by the number symbolism of the poem as
well. For example, the clerks search their libraries for seven days to
determine the corpse's identity. Their failure symbolizes the limitations
of man in this present life, which the number seven represents. On the
eighth day, St. Erkenwald receives the answer to his prayers and baptizes
the corpse. This is appropriate, for eight, associated with transformation
and renewal, became known as the baptismal number.[8] Whatley further
points out that historically, St. Erkenwald's feast was celebrated by a
liturgical octave (eight days of masses) by the three churches in the
London diocese most closely associated with the saint's cult. In addition,
at St. Paul's this octave coincided with the celebration of the Invention
of the Holy Cross, an interesting concurrence since St. Erkenwald is also
an invention (discovery) tale.[9]

One element of the poem which has not been much explored is the
relationship between the salvation of the pagan judge and Christ's descent
into Hell.[10] As we saw in Chapter II, these two issues are closely related,
for some theologians (especially the early Church Fathers) speculated on

---

[4]Benson 403.

[5]Lester L. Faigley,"Typology and Justice in *St. Erkenwald,*" *American Benedictine Review* 29 (1978): 384.

[6]Vincent F. Petronella, *"St. Erkenwald:* Style as the Vehicle for Meaning," *Journal of English and Germanic Philology* 66 (1967): 532–540.

[7]Arnold E. Davidson, "Mystery, Miracle, and Meaning in *St. Erkenwald,*" *Papers on Language and Literature* 16 (1979): 41–42; McAlindon 484; Reichardt 128–129; Cairns 437; Whatley, "Heathens" 340–342. In contrast to Whatley's emphasis on Erkenwald's ecclesiastical func-tion, Lally (8) suggests that the poem is actually a subtle criticism of the bishop's preoc-cupation with Church ritual.

[8]Reichardt 150 and Russell Peck, "Number Structure in *St. Erkenwald,*" *Annuale Mediaevale* 14 (1973): 10–12.

[9]Whatley, "Heathens" 277–278. See his article "The Middle English *St. Erkenwald* and Its Liturgical Context" for a full discussion of the links between the poem and the Cross legend.

[10]Ruth Morse (ed., *St. Erkenwald* [Totowa, N.J.: Rowman and Littlefield, 1975] 37) does mention in passing that "One reason for the pagan's salvation is implicit in the present situation, in which the people of the newly redeemed community need miraculous confir-mation of their belief. This also explains why the pagan was left behind at the Harrowing of Hell—not for his own sake but for the sake of others." Susan Clark and Julian Wasserman, in *"St. Erkenwald's* Spiritual Itinerary," *American Benedictine Review* 33 (1982): 264, 268–269, also mention briefly a connection with the Harrowing, which (like *St. Erkenwald*) combines apoc-alyptic themes with the concept of salvation for virtuous pagans.

the possibility that Christ had harrowed not only the Old Testament patriarchs and prophets but also the virtuous pagans. Indeed, as we have seen, many medieval theologians (in particular, Aquinas and the four-teenth-century "Pelagians") would not necessarily relegate the poem's upright judge to Hell. Erkenwald himself is obviously surprised to learn of this soul's damnation, as his comments indicate:

He þat rewardes vche a renke as he has riȝt seruyd
Myȝt euel forgo the to gyfe of His grace summe brawnche,
....
For þi say me of þi soule in sele quere ho wonnes
And of þe riche restorment þat raȝt hyr oure Lorde.[11]

In light of the general expectations of the time, then, *St. Erkenwald* can be read as the tale of a virtuous pagan deliberately left behind during the Harrowing to serve as an object lesson for later Christians.[12] It is this lesson, which may be examined in three parts, which is the purpose of the work as a hagiographic tale.

First, the poem reminds us of the essential characteristics of the Har-rowing. The event is of central importance as the great turning point in divine history from justice to mercy. The poet reminds us of his poem's link with the establishment of Christendom, for this miracle occurs shortly after the Crucifixion (l. 2)—a deliberate telescoping of chronology for thematic emphasis. In addition, we are reminded that the Crucifixion began the era of the New Covenant, the New Law of mercy which Christ introduced, by the poet's choice of terms: the characters of this tale live in "New Troy" and are engaged in building a "New Werke."

These terms have, of course, other connotations as well. For example, referring to London as "New Troy" is a reminder of Britain's legendary link with the Roman Empire. We remember that Dante especially stressed the importance of the Roman Empire in God's plan, for divine providence created the conditions under which the Incarnation would take place. Thus "New Troy" should remind us of God's all-knowing providence which, as the poem proves, comes into play again.[13] "New Werke" also has an historical basis; Savage notes that the term is an anachronism,

---

[11]Lines 275–276 and 279–280 of Peterson's edition of *St. Erkenwald.* Subsequent references to this work will be placed in parentheses within the text.

[12]This idea is supported by Aquinas, who implied that Trajan was just one of many who may have been damned in order to be later recalled to life:

De facto Traiani hoc modo potest probabiliter aestimari, quod precibus B. Gregorii ad vitam fuerit revocatus, et ita gratiam consecutus sit, per quam remissionem peccatorum habuit, et per consequens immunitatem a poena: sicut etiam apparet in omnibus illis qui fuerunt miraculose a mortuis suscitati, quorum plures constat idololatras et damnatos fuisse. De omnibus talibus enim similiter dici oportet quod non erant in inferno finaliter deputati, sed secundum praesentem propriorum meritorum iustitiam: secundum autem superiores causas, quibus praevidebantur ad vitam revocandi, erat aliter de eis disponendum.

(*Summa Theologica,* III [Supp.], LXXIV, V, ad 5)

[13]Whatley ("Heathens" 346, n. 46) notes that during the late 1300s, some Londoners did want to revive the ancient name of "New Troy" for their city.

though, for at the time the poet wrote, St. Erkenwald's tomb was located in the "New Work" begun in 1251.[14] Reichardt suggests a thematic interpretation for this term, pointing out that the phrase implies the "new creation" which results from conversion to Christianity, the process the judge will undergo. He links this to the scriptural metaphor of the temple to signify the human body, which is cleansed by baptism as this temple is being purged of paganism: "Þen was hit abatyd and beten doun and buggyd efte new" (l. 37).[15] In any event, it seems likely that the poet was aware of the scriptural connotations of the word "new" and appropriately chose to make use of them in the tale of a pagan who was damned under the Old Law but received mercy under the New.

The poem also reminds us of an important consequence of the Harrowing, the establishment of Christ's sovereignty over Hell. In this regard, the temple's name, the Triapolitan (which has no known historical basis), may refer to the three-tiered universe of heaven, earth, and hell which would be familiar to the medieval mind. For example, the King James version of Philippians 2:10 tells us "That at the name of Jesus every knee should bow, of things in heaven, and things in earth, and things under the earth." Earth was pictured as the center of the universe, with hell below and heaven above it. The corpse himself indicates this cosmological scheme: "Al heuen and helle . . . and erthe bitwene" (l. 196).

The poem's masons, then, are properly engaged in seeking the foundations of the church (ll. 41–42), for unless this is rebuilt they cannot proceed with the New Werke. In the same way, the New Work of the Church would not proceed until Christ descended to the foundation of the universe, Hell, and made Himself master there. This correlation is enhanced by the information in ll. 27–30 that the Triapolitan was previously owned by a "maghty devil," "the dryghtyn derrest of ydols praysid." Faigley points out the nice similarity between the human and the divine schemes: "The pagan judge is discovered in the foundation of an old temple that the 'New Werke' is to be built upon, which is precisely the relationship of the Old and New Laws—the New Law supplementing instead of supplanting the Old Law."[16]

We saw that in one version of the Gospel of Nicodemus Christ left His cross behind in Hell in order to save any souls inadvertently left behind, or perhaps to enable special pardons. It is tempting to put the judge into the category of souls rescued after the Harrowing by virtue of that cross, for he makes clear that he was an eye-witness to the Harrowing but not a participant in it:

I was non of þe nommbre þat þou wyt noy boghtes,

---

[14] Savage 27, n. 38.

[15] Reichardt 105, 107.

[16] Faigley 385. Clark and Wasserman (257–261) point out the poem's simultaneous manipulation of time and space, superimposing a tripartite scheme of past/present/future upon a tripartite cosmology of heaven/earth/hell.

Wyt þe blode of thi body vpon þe blo rode;
Quen þou herghedes helle-hole and hentes hom þeroute,
Þi loffynge oute of limbo, þou laftes me þer.

(ll. 289–292)

The corpse leaves ambiguous the fate of other pagans, but his words give
us the sense that he feels abandoned, a solitary sufferer "dwynande in
þe derke dethe" (l. 294). Yet his soul seems to dwell in Abraham's
bosom, or paradise (the upper region or "waiting room" of Hell), since
he suffers separation from God but does not mention any positive punishment.

The periphrasis "þe prince þat paradis weldes" (l. 161) reminds us
that Christ rules even here, and the poem demonstrates this when Erkenwald, acting as a surrogate of Christ, harrows this soul as a bishop
empowered by Him. Through this act, the universal sovereignty of Christ
is confirmed. He remains Master of Hell, for He can remove souls at will
from Satan's domain; He remains Master of earth, for He is served by
men such as Erkenwald who turn to Him in times of crisis; He remains
Master of Heaven, for the judge's soul talks of its reception into that
glory.

As a corollary of this, the poem confirms Christ as Minister of the
Sacraments. Reichardt points out that in the scene of the baptism, the
bishop is referred to as a "lede," a diminution of his earlier stature in the
poem. For example, in ll. 105–108 he is referred to as "byschop," "pri-
mate," and "Ser"—words which emphasize his superior station in life.[17]
The term "lede" implies that Erkenwald is simply a member of the human
species, indistinguishable from the "pepul."[18] The scene serves as a refutation of the Donatist heresy against which Augustine battled. Augustine argued that Christ, not the human agent, is the real minister of the
Church sacraments; thus sacraments administered by impure priests retained their efficacy.[19] Here the opposite point is made: even one of the
best of priests, a man worthy to follow in the footsteps of Gregory and
Augustine, is helpless to save the soul which he pities. The tears he sheds
are mere drops of water, but the names he invokes—"I folwe þe in þe
Fader nome and His fre Childes, / And of þe gracious Holy Goste" (ll.
317–318)—work a miracle.

The poem's second major lesson involves the illustration of the function
and presence of each Member of the Trinity. (In this respect, the "tri"
of the name Triapolitan may refer to the three members of the Godhead.[20])

---

[17]Reichardt 61.

[18]Reichardt 137. Lally makes the point that Erkenwald's abandonment of his official role
leads to the miracle: "his greatest moment is one of greatest humility" (8).

[19]Reichardt 136–138.

[20]Savage, however, endorses Gollancz's explanation that the word signifies a trinity of
metropolitan cities (24–25, n. 31). Morse (66, note to l. 31) suggests that since London,
York, and Canterbury were the three most important ecclesiastical centers in medieval
England, the poet may have invented "triapolitanes" to suggest a similar pagan hierarchy.

The judge, living under the Old Law before the Incarnation, is himself judged with strict severity and consigned to Hell as a result of original sin. This function of uncompromising justice was traditionally associated with God the Father, the Yahweh of the Old Testament. With the Incarnation, Christ ushered in a new era of mercy and charity. This was signaled by the Harrowing of Hell, for the deliverance of these souls was the first effect of the Crucifixion. Thus the specific reference to the Harrowing, the actual harrowing of this soul, and the compassion evoked in Erkenwald and the spectators witness the presence of Christ as the second Member of the Trinity. Finally, the presence of the Holy Spirit is proven by the efficacy of Erkenwald's tears and the references to the heavenly supper awaiting the soul released from Hell. Through the action of the Spirit, water becomes spiritually cleansing, and bread and wine become body and blood. The Spirit is also present in the corpse's very act of speaking. Although the runes on the coffin could not be deciphered, even by clerks "wyt crownes ful brode" (l. 55), the corpse speaks in the language native to the onlookers. This is reminiscent of the Spirit at Pentecost, which enabled the apostles to speak in unknown tongues.[21] The poet even tells us that the corpse speaks "Þurghe sum Goste lant lyfe of hym þat al redes" (l. 192). With these references to the Holy Spirit in mind, we can appreciate the relevance of the special mass celebrated earlier by St. Erkenwald. The opening words, "Spiritus Domini" (l. 132), identify this as the Votive Mass of the Holy Spirit, emphasizing praise to the Spirit for grace.[22]

The third and most significant lesson of the work, however, is directly related to the issue of the virtuous pagan. The judge's plight brings to mind the religious controversies of the fourteenth century which we examined earlier, with the emphasis here on the Bradwardinian view that human achievement can never merit salvation. Indeed, Whatley goes so far as to claim that the *Erkenwald*-poet deliberately altered the details of the Gregory/Trajan legend in order to discredit "the liberal scholastic theology concerning the righteous heathen in general" and perhaps to respond to "the radicalism of Langland and Wyclif" in their presentation of the Trajan legend.[23]

---

[21]William Hutchings, "'The Unintelligible Terms of an Incomprehensible Damnation': Samuel Beckett's *The Unnamable, Skeol,* and *St. Erkenwald,*" *Twentieth Century Literature* 27 (Summer 1981): 108–109. But as Whatley points out ("Heathens" 350), we are never told the meaning of the "roynyshe" writing on the coffin.

[22]Morse 69, note to l. 132.

[23]Whatley, "Heathens" 345. Whatley goes on to contend that the poet calls into question the liberal view of pagan salvation "to discourage or dispel the notion entertained by not a few of his contemporaries that the moral life of the individual in society counted for more, *sub specie aeternitatis,* than his participation in the sacramental life of the church" (346). In keeping with this objective, the poet takes care to distinguish Erkenwald from the Gregory of the early biographers and of the contemporary humanists; Erkenwald "is untainted by any suggestion of unorthodoxy or heroic individualism and is much more obviously the embodiment of traditional, ecclesiastical Christianity" (353).

The "Pelagians" of the time would have expected this soul to be in heaven, for the judge had done his best to live a virtuous life. This is amply attested to by the honors with which he was buried and by God's intervention to preserve his body as a token of unusual virtue. Yet this was *natural* virtue, apparently sufficient to preserve his flesh but not his soul. As soon as the judge receives supernatural grace, his body rots—an indication of its relative importance in the divine scheme. As Ruth Morse puts it,

It is a splendid touch that salvation is immediately followed by bodily dissolution: everyone had thought that the preservation of the 'ferly' was the miracle, but the true miracle was the salvation of the heathen, to which the wonder was the means.[24]

This soul, left behind during Christ's Harrowing, seems to have been singled out by God for His special purposes. This is true whether we think of the judge as one pagan rescued from a crowded Limbo or as one pagan somehow left behind in a deserted Limbo. The poet, however, seems to indicate the latter possibility, which makes emphatic the Bradwardinian view: not that only the most righteous pagan could be rescued from Hell, but that *even* the most righteous pagan could in all justice be left behind because of the taint of original sin. The judge knows that he was left behind because he lacks the "medecyn" for original sin, "Þat is, fulloght in fonte wyt faitheful bileue" (l. 299). Since none of the souls in Limbo would have received baptism before the time of the Harrowing, this implies that Christ descended to baptize those He would deliver. Somehow, the judge intimates, he was overlooked; yet he neither berates Christ for passing over him nor questions why he was singled out to be left behind. This is in keeping with his reputation as "Þe kidde kynge of kene iustices" (l. 254): in all justice, he has no claim to salvation. Although he had no opportunity to learn of Christ (as he reminds us in a prayer of mild protest in ll. 285–288), he realizes that the blame rests on Adam, "Þat ete of Þat appulle / Þat mony a plyȝtles pepul has poysned for euer" (ll. 294–295), not on Christ. Erkenwald's sermon, which stresses the chasm between human reason and divine revelation, also indicates the powerlessness of man before original sin:

Bot quen matyd is monnes myȝt and his mynde passyde,
And al his resons are to-rent and redeles he stondes,
Þen lettes hit Hym ful litelle to louse wyt a fynger
Þat alle Þe hondes vnder heuen halde myȝt neuer.
                    (ll. 163–166)

Thus the poet underlines the poem's primary message, man's absolute necessity of grace, in two ways. First, it is not the judge's own merit which saves him if his companions have already been delivered from Hell;

---

[24]Morse 39.

rather, he is saved through grace alone. In addition, the poem brings together the most just and the most holy of men, but neither the judge's good works nor the bishop's pity can suffice for salvation. Instead, we are forced to recognize that, in the words of the *Pearl*-poet, "the grace of God is gret innoghe."[25] Furthermore, that grace must be received by baptism, in accordance with God's *potentia ordinata*.[26]

The lessons of the poem are further reinforced by the symbolism of the numbers three and eight. The presence of the Trinity in the climactic scene, as well as the implicit and explicit references to the three-tiered universe, suggests the importance of the number three. Three and eight are linked, for, besides one, eight is the only cube (a number raised to the *third* power) among the primary numbers. Thus the Trinity (three in one) leads all the characters in the poem to the cleansing and renewal signified by the number eight. In addition, the poem's second most dominant motif, justice, is also associated with eight; the cube, with its equal sides and surfaces, was seen as a model of equability.[27] And baptism, performed in the name of the Trinity, usually took place in an octagonal baptismal font, here provided by the shape of the poem itself (eight alliterative quatrains followed by an exposition of the miracle in 80 stanzas, the whole poem being 88 stanzas long).[28]

In conclusion, *St. Erkenwald* is a poem which demonstrates that a pagan can be saved, but not through his own merit. An absolute essential is grace, signified here by baptism. This grace was made possible by the Harrowing, which established Christ's sovereignty over all levels of the universe and made possible the transition from the Father's justice to Christ's mercy, still accessible to man through the Holy Spirit. Thus the poem can be seem as a reminder and celebration of the New Covenant (or "New Work") which, thanks to Christ's sacrifice, is offered to all— those living before the Incarnation as well as after. The poem's miracle, the "harrowing in miniature," recalls the great division between justice and mercy in Christian history and holds up faithful priests such as Erkenwald who carry on the Church's new ministry of charity. (As we shall see, *Piers Plowman* emphasizes the same temporal divisions, but with a decidedly less optimistic view.)

In addition, the poem serves as a message to the fourteenth-century Church. Except for the judge, no one in *St. Erkenwald* is actually converted to Christianity; rather, they are steadied and strengthened in their faith.

---

[25]Although their common authorship is far from certain, it is interesting to note that baptism in both *The Pearl* and *St. Erkenwald* is an absolute requirement for salvation; neither an infant's innocence nor perfect righteousness will alone suffice.

[26]The poet does achieve a balance of sorts between the standpoints of Bradwardine and the Pelagians. Although the judge *must* receive salvation through divine grace in the sacrament of baptism, the basis of the miracle itself lies in his own merit, his own reputation for justice.

[27]Peck 13.

[28]Peck 21, 10.

This is signified by the change in the people from an unruly crowd that "suche a cry aboute a cors, crakit euer-more" (l. 110) to the orderly, loving procession of the final quatrain. With this in mind, we can view the poem as delivering an imperative to the Church: Christians must continue the work of "harrowing," or delivering souls from the threat of Hell, a directive which is true in at least two senses. If, as the poem teaches, neither good works nor reason alone is sufficient for salvation, then the Church must actively seek to convert and baptize unbelievers. Furthermore, the Church must cleanse itself, both collectively and individually, of all elements which would hinder the "New Work" effected by Christ's intervention on man's behalf.

In short, the miracle vivifies the need for divine aid on behalf of individuals and the Church as a whole; man's tears are as useless as the judge's righteousness if not supplemented by the efficacy of grace. The poet uplifts his audience, however, by showing that Christ's bishops, as exemplified by Erkenwald, are holy, worthy men and that Providence— which can even hold a soul in reserve for a special purpose—can be trusted.

V. *PIERS PLOWMAN*: ISSUES IN SALVATION AND THE HARROWING AS THEMATIC CLIMAX

*P*iers Plowman is a fourteenth-century poem which continues to resist all attempts to unlock its design. It does not fit neatly into any medieval genre, and even the goal of the Dreamer's quest—the most basic element of the work—is a matter of debate.[1] Another crux which continues to elicit conjecture is the meaning of the terms Dowel, Dobet, and Dobest which are used to divide the poem into sections. While I do not pretend to possess *the* key to Piers Plowman, some of its baffling elements can be profitably examined through a study of the poem's climactic scene—the Harrowing of Hell—and the theological discussions which involve such related issues as the fate of pagans, the necessity of baptism, and the efficacy of good works and learning.

---

[1] Charles Muscatine discusses the difficulty of placing *Piers Plowman* in any genre on pp. 73–106 of *Poetry and Crisis in the Age of Chaucer* (Notre Dame: University of Notre Dame Press, 1972). He reaches a summary conclusion:

The obscurity of the larger plan, the seemingly capricious interplay of debate, pilgrimage, and quest, and of mimetics and didacticism; the periodic establishment and collapse of the dream-frame; the shiftiness of space; the paradox of graphic power and pictorial diffuseness; the alternations within a great range of tone and temper; the shiftiness of rhythm—all these produce a curiously homogeneous artistic effect that for lack of a better term I have called surrealistic. (106)

Morton Bloomfield (*Piers Plowman as a Fourteenth Century Apocalypse* [New Brunswick, N.J.: Rutgers University Press, 1962] 22–23 and 32–33) also tackles this problem by associating the poem with three literary genres and three religious genres.

On the purpose of the Dreamer's quest, critical opinion tends to divide between salvation (most notably, Robert Worth Frank, Jr., *Piers Plowman and the Scheme of Salvation: An Interpretation of Dowel, Dobet and Dobest*, Yale Studies in English 136 [New Haven, Conn.: Yale University Press, 1957] and John Lawlor, *Piers Plowman: An Essay in Criticism* [New York: Barnes and Noble, 1962]) and spiritual perfection (especially Edward Vasta, *The Spiritual Basis of Piers Plowman*, Studies in English 18 [New York: Humanities Press, 1965] and Bloomfield, *Apocalypse*).

Some of the seminal arguments which attempt to organize *Piers Plowman* through identification of Dowel, Dobet, and Dobest are as follows: Henry W. Wells, "The Construction of *Piers Plowman*," *PMLA* 44 (1929): 123–140; Nevill Coghill, "The Character of Piers Plowman Considered from the B Text," *Medium Aevum* 2 (1933): 108–135; R. W. Chambers, *Man's Unconquerable Mind* (London: Jonathan Cape, 1939) 88–171. Wells, Coghill, and Chambers argue that the three "Do's" correspond to active, contemplative, and mixed lives respectively.

Two critics have contended that the three lives are the mystic's purgative, illuminative, and unitive states: Howard Meroney, "The Life and Death of Longe Wille," *English Literary History* 17 (1950): 1–35; E. Talbot Donaldson, *Piers Plowman: The C-Text and Its Poet* (New Haven: Yale University Press, 1949), esp. 156–161.

In addition, a useful summary of this and other questions can be found in Morton Bloomfield's article, "Present State of *Piers Plowman* Studies," *Speculum* 14 (1939): 215–232. A more recent and more comprehensive review is that of John Raymond McCully, Jr., "Conceptions of *Piers Plowman*: 1550 to 1970's," Ph.D. diss., Rice University 1976.

Because *Piers Plowman* is undoubtedly a theological poem (although written in the vernacular and possibly intended for lay as well as clerical
audiences[2]), it seems logical to approach the poem through a study of the
theological issues it addresses in light of fourteenth-century thought. One
attempt to do this is Ruth Ames' *The Fulfillment of the Scriptures: Abraham,
Moses, and Piers;* she reads the work as an exemplification of how the Old
Testament is fulfilled by the New, an orthodox view given special emphasis during the Middle Ages through the use of typology.[3] Morton
Bloomfield, however, sees the poem as the product of an older, more
monastic tradition, concerned more with social than individual regeneration.[4] Specifically, he places the poem in the English Franciscan tradition.[5]
Daniel Murtaugh, in *Piers Plowman and the Image of God,* takes yet another
approach. Using the medieval idea of man as the image of God, he traces
through the poem the connections between divinity and humanity, connections which Langland demonstrates primarily in the social and intellectual realms.[6] Perhaps two of the most valiant attempts to place the
poem in its religious context are Greta Hort's *Piers Plowman and Contemporary
Thought* and *Piers Plowman and Scriptural Tradition* by D.W. Robertson, Jr., and
Bernard F. Huppé. Both works suffer, however, because they face the
near-impossible task of analyzing the entire poem, in all of its diffuse
complexity, from a theological standpoint.[7]

---

[2] John Burrow ("The Audience of *Piers Plowman,*" *Anglia* 75 [1957]: 373–384) contends
that, based on the large number of surviving manuscripts, *Piers Plowman* reached not only a
clerical audience but also a new audience of "prosperous, literate laymen" (378). Sister
Carmeline Sullivan (*The Latin Insertions and the Macaronic Verse in Piers Plowman* [Washington,
D.C.: Catholic University of America Press, 1932] 62) agrees that the poem was designed
for laymen as well as clerics, based on the large number of Latin quotations which Langland
paraphrased, explained, or translated. Bloomfield (*Apocalypse* 42), however, urges caution in
extending the bounds of the audience: "It is hard to think of a large, popular audience for
the work, in spite of John Ball's reference to *Piers* in his famous letter of 1381. The poem
is too difficult and too allusive to have been enjoyed by the common people or by restless,
uprooted clerics. The references to Piers and the poems influenced by it all argue for a
medium-sized, literate, thoughtful audience."

[3] Ruth M. Ames, *The Fulfillment of the Scriptures: Abraham, Moses, and Piers* (Evanston, Ill.:
Northwestern University Press, 1970). For a general introduction of the concept of typology
in theology, see James Barr, "Allegory and Typology," in *A New Dictionary of Christian Theology,*
ed. Alan Richardson and John Bowden, 1983 ed.

[4] Bloomfield, *Apocalypse* vii-4.

[5] Bloomfield, *Apocalypse* 162. See also Mother Catherine Elizabeth Maguire, R.S.C.J., "Franciscan Elements in the Thought of *Piers Plowman,*" Ph.D. diss., Fordham University 1950.
Sister Rose Bernard Donna has tackled the poem in a similar way in *Despair and Hope: A
Study in Langland and Augustine* (Washington, D.C.: Catholic University of America Press,
1948).

[6] Daniel M. Murtaugh, *Piers Plowman and the Image of God* (Gainesville: University of Florida
Press, 1978).

[7] Greta Hort (*Piers Plowman and Contemporary Religious Thought* [New York: Macmillan, 1937])
establishes the theological works Langland was most likely familiar with and then attempts
to define the poem's stand on the attributes of man, the issue of predestination, and the
meaning of the Atonement and sacrament of penance. Taking a completely different approach, D. W. Robertson, Jr., and Bernard Huppé (*Piers Plowman and Scriptural Tradition* [Prin-
ceton, N.J.: Princeton University Press, 1951]) present a detailed explication of the poem,
with an eye to exposing each of the four levels of allegory. Both works have been subjected

Other critics have been more successful by limiting their focus to a specific issue or a specific context of the poem, and it is in their footsteps that my treatment follows. In particular, several studies concentrate on the issue of the virtuous pagan and/or the larger issue of the relative merits of grace vs. works. M.E. Marcett has identified the hypocritical friar of the banquet scene (C. XVI) as Friar William Jordan, who became involved in a controversy with Uthred of Boldon, the espouser of the theory of a *clara visio* granted each individual at the moment of death.[8] This theory, although condemned in 1368, solved the dilemma of the fate of those who had died without Christian baptism. Marcett's identification is accepted by G.H. Russell, who attempts to prove Uthred's influence on *Piers Plowman* through examining revisions of pertinent passages (especially those relating to baptism) in the A, B, and C texts.[9] Earlier, R.W. Chambers had become interested in the same theme, pointing out that the B-text plunges into the problems of predestination and the salvation of the righteous heathen which the A-text had left unanswered. Chambers contends that the author abandoned the A-text for fifteen years because he was conscious of his solitary stand on the possibility of salvation for pagans: "He believes that he has against him the opinion of all learned men."[10] Subsequent studies, however, have proven that the author's concern with the fate of virtuous pagans was part of a larger debate about the roles of grace and good works in salvation.[11] As we have seen, the

---

to rather sharp criticism. Bloomfield (*Studies* 232, n. 6) accuses Hort of ignoring much of the scholarship of *Piers Plowman,* resulting in error or duplication. For examples of the negative reactions provoked by Robertson and Huppé's work, see the reviews by Morton Bloomfield in *Speculum* 27 (1952): 245–249; Randolph Quirk, *Journal of English and Germanic Philology* 52 (1953): 253–255; and T. P. Dunning, *Medium Aevum* 24 (1955): 23–29.

[8] M. E. Marcett, *Uhtred of Boldon, Friar William Jordan and Piers Plowman* (New York: The Author, 1938).

[9] G.H. Russell, "The Salvation of the Heathen: The Exploration of a Theme in *Piers Plowman,*" *Journal of the Warburg and Courtauld Institute* 29 (1966): 101–116.

[10] R.W. Chambers, "Long Will, Dante, and the Righteous Heathen," *Essays and Studies by Members of the English Association* 9 (1924): 68.

[11] See, for example, Janet Coleman, *"Sublimes et Litterati:* The Audience for the Themes of Grace, Justification, and Predestination, Traced from the Disputes of the Fourteenth-Century *Moderni* to the Vernacular *Piers Plowman,*" Ph.D. diss., Yale University 1970; and John F. McNamara, "Responses to Ockhamist Theology in the Poetry of the *Pearl* -Poet, Langland, and Chaucer," Ph.D. diss., Louisiana State University 1968. (Janet Coleman has since published *Piers Plowman and the Moderni* [Rome: Edizioni di storia e letteratura, 1981].)

In addition, several articles attempting to prove Langland's emphasis either on grace or works have recently been published. Gordon Whatley, in "The Uses of Hagiography: The Legend of Pope Gregory and the Emperor Trajan in the Middle Ages" (*Viator* 15 [1984]: 50–56) states that Langland's Trajan was saved by a "mysterious combination of faithful justice and divine grace" (55), but the thrust of his article is that Trajan's works, especially in contrast to the "dead letter of ecclesiastical formalism" (55) were primary. Pamela Gradon ("*Trajanus redivivus:* Another Look at Trajan in *Piers Plowman,*" in *Middle English Studies Presented to Norman Davis in Honor of His Seventieth Birthday,* ed. Douglas Gray and E. G. Stanley [Oxford: Clarendon Press, 1983] 93–114) likewise argues for the prevalence of works. In her view, the poem answers affirmatively the question of whether man can be saved *ex puris naturalibus.* Robert Adams, in "Piers's Pardon and Langland's Semi-Pelagianism" (*Traditio* 39 [1983]: 367–418) also traces Langland's emphasis on works, or doing one's best (*facere quod in se est*), through several passages in the poem. Denise Baker, exploring the same issues in "From

theologians of the fourteenth century were divided on this issue: those who followed Bradwardine emphasized the primacy of grace and the futility of man's efforts toward salvation; those who opposed Bradwardine, the Pelagians, contended that man could dispose himself to receive saving grace through merit *de congruo;* and those few who attempted a precarious moderate stand between the two extremes dwelt on the co-operation of grace and works.

Although the present work also deals with the theme of the virtuous pagan in *Piers Plowman,* it differs from the above studies in some respects. First, it deals almost exclusively with the C-text, accepting it as Langland's final revision and, more importantly, as the text most concerned with the elaboration of theological issues.[12] Second, I am not attempting to examine the influence of a particular figure such as Uthred of Boldon nor to place the poem or its poet in any specific theological camp. Rather, with the given theological climate in mind as the poem's context, I intend to examine the author's use of the idea of the virtuous pagan. This concept is reflected in the poem's discussion of such issues as the importance of baptism and learning for salvation and the idea of different degrees of reward. In addition, a central focus of the poem is Christ's Harrowing of Hell, an event closely associated with the issue of the virtuous pagan since, strictly speaking, those He harrowed were pagans. Christ's mastery of Hell and His deliverance of its captives marked the turning point from

---

Plowing to Penitence: *Piers Plowman* and Fourteenth Century Theology," *Speculum* 55 (1980): 715–725, and in "Dialectic Form in *Pearl* and *Piers Plowman,*" *Viator* 15 (1984): 263–273, comes to the opposite conclusion: "Langland agrees with the *Pearl* poet: the righteous are indeed saved, but they are saved by grace" ("Dialectic" 269). Janet Coleman (*Medieval Readers and Writers 1350–1400* [New York: Columbia University Press, 1981] 251–252), while taking a more moderate position than Baker, does see in the C-text a comparatively greater emphasis on grace, "a movement away from the more radical ethic of Ockham and Holcot, which emphasizes salvation through good works performed naturally, to an emphasis similar to Wyclif's, on the activity of God's will in granting the grace that saves."

Using a different strategy, Samuel A. Overstreet, in " 'Grammaticus Ludens': Theological Aspects of Langland's Grammatical Allegory" (*Traditio* 40 [1984]: 252–296), approaches the question through an examination of the terms *mede, mercede, relacion rect* and *indirect* in the notoriously obscure passage in Passus 3, lines 290–405. Murtaugh (44–49) and Coleman (*Medieval Readers* 252–259) tackle the same passage.

[12] Although the authorship controversy is still not definitively settled, it has little effect here. I accept the majority opinion favoring single authorship (especially in light of George Kane's work, *Piers Plowman: The Evidence for Authorship* [London: Athlone Press, 1965]) and use "Langland" as a convenient designation rather than as an argument for a single author, since biographical details will not enter into my discussion of the poem. The validity of the C-text as the best choice for an examination of the poet's theology is supported by Sister Carmeline Sullivan, who examines the progressive amplification of Latin verses in the A, B, and C versions, concluding of C that "It was Langland's last chance to speak his mind, so he tried to leave nothing untold" (47). Quotations from the C-text will come from Walter W. Skeat's edition (London: Oxford University Press, 1886); references to the poem will be placed in parentheses within the text. I have chosen to use Skeat's edition for the convenience of comparison with the A and B versions; however, I have also compared Skeat's text with that of Derek Pearsall, ed., *Piers Plowman by William Langland: An Edition of the C-text* (Berkeley and Los Angeles: University of California Press, 1979) and have relied heavily on Pearsall's excellent notes.

justice to mercy, from the hopeless damnation of paganism to the hope
of eternal life in Christ. The structure of *Piers Plowman* reflects the importance of this event by delineating three distinct epochs of divine history: the Old Testament dispensation of strict justice; the time of Christ,
especially the action of the Harrowing; and the reign (and impending
collapse) of the Church Militant.

Let us begin with an examination of the relevant theological issues
debated in the *Dowel* section of the poem, which depicts the Dreamer's
intellectual and psychological progress.[13] As we shall see, *Dowel* appears
to follow the general method of scholastic argument, so that we are first
introduced to two sides of a question and later given a solution which
attempts to include and reconcile both sides.[14] (The Harrowing itself does
this as it includes and reconciles Old and New Covenants, justice and
mercy.) Three important questions posed in *Dowel* are (1) the importance
of baptism for salvation, (2) the place of learning in salvation, and (3)
degrees of reward.

Baptism, the first question, is dealt with primarily in Passus XIII, when
Scripture recounts the parable of the banquet to which many were called
but few chosen. The Dreamer fears for his own soul ("And in a weer
gan ich wexe and with my-selue to dispute / Whether ich were chose
other nat chose"; XIII. 50–51), but then reassures himself that his baptism
irrevocably marks him as one of the chosen: "For thauh a Crystine man
coueytede hus Crystendome to reneye, / Ryghtfulliche to reneye no
reson hit wolde" (XIII. 59–60). Although a Christian might deserve purgatory, in the "day of dome" he would receive "mercy for hus mysdedes"
(XIII. 68–70). Scripture agrees that "may no synne lette / Mercy, that
hue nel al amende yf meeknesse here folwe" (XIII. 71–72).

The word "meeknesse" evidently serves as a wedge to introduce
Trajan—as we have seen, the virtuous pagan *par excellence* for the Middle
Ages, and reputed for his great humility. But his speech does not show
meekness; rather, he interjects a counter-argument on the question of
baptism. The Dreamer has just claimed that his Christian baptism will
assure him of salvation; Trajan, however, puts forth his own case of
salvation without baptism—indeed, without any specific Christian belief.
He merited salvation because he fulfilled the imperatives of the Old and
New Covenants—both justice and love: "Loue, withoute leel by-leyue

[13] Sister Mary C. Davlin O.P. ("*Kynde Knowyng* as a Major Theme in *Piers Plowman B,*" *Review
of English Studies,* n.s. 22 [1971]: 3) suggests that the Dreamer's quest for intellectual knowledge
in *Dowel* renders his allusions to *kynde knowyng* ironical. Given Holychurche's praise of *kynde
knowyng* in I. 142–144, it is conceivable that most, if not all, of the Dreamer's efforts in
Dowel are ironic, as he constantly attempts to substitute theory for action. (See, in this regard,
John Lawlor's essay "The Imaginative Unity of *Piers Plowman,*" in *Style and Symbolism in Piers
Plowman,* ed. Robert J. Blanch [Knoxville, Tenn.: University of Tennessee Press, 1969] 101–
116.)

[14] Hort 39–40. Also see Philomena O'Driscoll, "The *Dowel* Debate in *Piers Plowman B,*"
Medium Aevum 50 (1981): 18–29. O'Driscoll argues that the poem builds up a synthesis
between faith and reason in the system-making tradition of Aquinas (27–28).

and my lawe ryghtful / Sauede me Sarrasyn soule and body bothe"
(XIII. 86–87). Elizabeth Kirk notes that even the form of his name,
Troianus, suggests the central quality of truth or troth, indicating that his
salvation is not an exception but a principle.[15]

Although he must acknowledge Gregory's role in his salvation ("he
wilnede wepynge that ich were saued," XIII. 82),[16] his total separation
from the sacraments is stressed: "With-oute moo bedes-byddyng hus
[Gregory's] bone was vnderfonge, / And ich ysaued, as ʒe may see
with-oute syngynge of masse" (XIII. 83–84). Langland's version of the
Trajan legend is unusual in that it does omit baptism; many analogues
of the tale relate Trajan's re-animation, at least long enough to receive
baptism.[17] This is, after all, the main point of *St. Erkenwald*—that even the
most upright judge cannot be saved unless he is a baptized Christian.

At this point we have two extreme positions expressed: a baptized
Christian must perforce be saved; but, on the other hand, baptism is not
a prerequisite for salvation. The scholastic presentation of the issue of
baptism, with two opposed extremes, leads us to expect a solution. And
in Passus XV Ymaginatif solves the dilemma with two answers, one
entirely orthodox and the other verging on Pelagianism. First, Ymaginatif
adopts Aquinas' argument that there is more than one kind of baptism:
"Ther is follyng of font and follyng in blod-shedynge, / And thorw
fuyr is follyng and al is ferm by-leyue" (XV. 207–208).[18] (In other words,
Ymaginatif asserts the validity of baptism at the font, through martyrdom,
and through the Holy Spirit.)

But Ymaginatif does not stop here. He presents an argument which
calls for the salvation of all virtuous men, regardless of their religious
beliefs:

Ac treuthe, that trespassede neuere ne transuered aʒens the lawe,
Bote lyuede as his lawe tauhte and leyueth ther be no bettere,
And yf ther were, he wolde and in suche a wil deyeth—
Wolde neuere trewe god bote trewe treuthe were a-lowed.
And where hit worth other nat worth the by-leyue is gret of treuthe,
And hope hongeth ay ther-on to haue that treuthe deserueth.   (XV. 209–214)

---

[15] Elizabeth D. Kirk, *The Dream Thought of Piers Plowman* (New Haven: Yale University Press, 1972) 135, n. 6.

[16] In the B-text, Gregory's role is even further minimized:

Nouʒt thorw preyere of a pope but for his pure treuthe
Was the Sarasene saued as seynt Gregorie bereth witnesse.   (B. XI, 150–151)

[17] See p. 42. Whatley uses these same points—Gregory's minimal role and Trajan's separation from the sacraments—to argue for Langland's anticlericalism ("Uses" 51–53).

[18] Aquinas, *Summa Theologica,* 3a, 66, 11. Pearsall notes that the concept of baptism by fire (Holy Spirit) provides "an interim answer which accommodates the story of Trajan and softens the ruthless predestinarianism of Bradwardine" (245, n. 208). Gradon, however, argues that Trajan's claims as to his own merits make it unlikely that he received any form of baptism (99).

Ymaginatif confirms Trajan's salvation ("Traianus was a trewe knyght
and took neuere Crystendome, / And he is saf, seith the bok and his
soule in heuene," XV. 205–206), with the implication that he was rewarded because he *facit quod in se est,* which is clearly the import of lines
209–214, and because of his extreme justness: *"uix saluabitur iustus in die
iudicii; / Ergo saluabitur"* (XV. 203–204). (This may also indicate how Piers
learned the way to Truth. His directions to the would-be pilgrims in the
Visio show that as a just man, he knew well the meaning of the Ten
Commandments but possessed only a dim recognition of Christian truths.)

If the poet's beliefs are voiced through Ymaginatif, we can assume that
he uses Trajan to prove that pagans can attain salvation. But he would
not, as Chambers believed, have been comforted by familiarity with *St.
Erkenwald* as another tale of pagan salvation.[19] *St. Erkenwald* illustrates the
absolute necessity of baptism for salvation; Langland, if he did not come
in contact with that work, was at least familiar with the traditional legend
of Trajan and deliberately dispensed with the pagan emperor's baptism.[20]
His point seems to be that Christian rituals avail nothing without works.

This does not mean that he would have his own non-Christian contemporaries continue in their ignorance. But he does show a great deal
of compassion for them, including them in the overall Christian scheme
("For Crist clepide ous alle come yf we wolde, / Sarrasyns and scis-
matikes and so he dude the Iewes," XIII. 53–54) and places much of the
blame for their condition on the Church itself:

Yf preest-hod were parfit and preyede thus the peuple sholde amende,
That now contrarien Cristes lawes and Cristendom despisen.
For sutthe that thes Sarasyns scribes, and thes Iewes
Hauen a lippe of oure by-leyue the lightloker, me thynketh,
Thei sholde turne, who so trauayle wolde and of the Trinite techen hem.(XVIII.
                                                                    250–254)[21]

A related question, the importance of learning in salvation, is taken up
in Passus XII, appropriately peopled by such characters as Wit, Study,
and Clergy. Two ideas are made clear: learning can be harmful if not
accompanied by use of the knowledge acquired; learning alone does not
guarantee salvation.

The first idea, the uselessness of learning in isolation, is made clear by
Study's rebuke of Wit (XII. 3) and Scripture's scowl upon Clergy (XII.
163–164) for wasting too much time in teaching Will, who shows no
disposition to make practical use of the knowledge he so zealously ac-
quires. He seeks knowledge not in a quest for *caritas* but merely to satisfy

---

[19] Chambers, "Long Will" 67–68.

[20] Russell (108–109) points out the changes from the B to C texts which make clear
Trajan's lack of baptism.

[21] An extended discussion of the topic of conversion can be found in Michael R. Paull's
"Mahomet and the Conversion of the Heathen in *Piers Plowman," English Language Notes* 10
(1972): 1–8.

his *curiosítas,* and he often becomes sidetracked by irrelevancies.[22] His misunderstanding of the proper use of knowledge is obvious from his basic grammatical error: he seeks to *find* Dowel, ignoring its imperative force and instead seeking for a non-existent substantive.[23] Study brings up Christ's injunction against such seekers: *"nolite mittere,* ӡe men margerie-perles / A-monge hogges that hauen hawes at wille" (XII. 7–8). Study further deplores the current abuse of learning: "He is reuerenced and robed that can robbe the peuple / Thorw fallas and false questes and thorw fykel speche" (XII. 21–22), while "he that hath holy writ aye in hus mouthe . . . Lytel is he a-lowed there-fore among lordes at festes" (XII. 31, 34). Interestingly, Study makes a distinction between human and divine knowledge. After listing the various fields she takes responsibility for—logic, music, poetry, grammar, and crafts (XII. 119–128)— she admits:

Ac Theologie hath teened me ten score tymes,
The more ich muse ther-on the mystiloker hit semeth,
And the deppere ich deuyne the derker me thynketh hit.   (XII. 129–131)

Then, as the Fathers made a clear distinction between philosophy and faith, she adds: "Hit is no science sothliche bote a sothfast by-leyue" (XII. 132). This is another way of expressing the uselessness of mere *scientia,* which is of a different order altogether—although, as Ymaginatif later implies, it can be a useful building-block to faith (XV. 193–199).

We saw that, on the question of salvation, the Dreamer became concerned when Scripture informed him that many were called but few chosen. Likewise, in relation to learning, Scripture tells him, *"multi multa sapiunt, et seipsos nesciunt"* (XII. 165). These words, which drive home the futility of knowledge sought purely for its own sake, catapult the Dreamer into a state of recklessness, embodied by a separate character of that name.[24] In this guise, he expresses an extreme position which Ymaginatif will later moderate, the idea that learning avails nothing due to predestination:

Go ich to helle, go ich to heuene ich shal nouht go myn one!
. . . .

---

[22] David Mills, "The Role of the Dreamer in *Piers Plowman,*" in *Piers Plowman: Critical Approaches,* ed. S.S. Hussey (London: Methuen and Co., Ltd., 1969) 209. Mills also points out the contrast between the Dreamer's thought and withdrawal and Piers' action and involvement in the poem. In addition, see Lawlor, "Imaginative Unity" 101–116 and John M. Bowers, *The Crisis of Will in Piers Plowman* (Washington, D.C.: Catholic University of America Press, 1986). Bowers devotes the greater part of his book to a study of *acedia* in *Piers Plowman.*

[23] Mills 195. Mary Carruthers (*The Search for St. Truth: A Study of Meaning in Piers Plowman* [Evanston, Illinois: Northwestern University Press, 1973] 89) also points out that "one doesn't explain Dowel, one does well." Will's "grammatical misperception of Dowel" and his "overly intellectual approach" are made clear by Trajan, the exemplar of the active life of Dowel (97).

[24] Donaldson 174.

For Clergie seith that he seih in the seynt euangelie,
That ich man maked was and my name y-entred
In the legende of life longe er ich were.
Predestinat thei prechen prechours that this shewen,
Or prechen inparfit ypult out of grace.
(XII. 200, 204–208)

As examples of the futility of learning, Rechlessnesse cites Solomon and Aristotle, held by tradition to be in Hell[25]:

For Salomon the sage that Sapience made,
God gaf hym grace of wit and of good after,
Neuere to man so muche that man can of telle,
To rewele alle reames and ryche to make,
And deme wel and wislyche wommen bereth witnesse; *Non michi nec tibi, sed diuidatur.*
Aristotle and he hij tauhten men bothe;
Maisters that techen men of godes muchel mercy
Witnessen that here wordes and here werkes both
Weren wonder goode and wise in here tyme,
And holychurche, as ich huyre haldeth bothe in helle!   (XII.211–220)

If we accept Rechlessnesse as an external embodiment of the Dreamer's state of mind, we see the irony of his choice of examples. As Joseph Wittig puts it, "He seizes upon Solomon and Aristotle, whom tradition has damned, arguing that their knowledge availed them nothing—a point his informants have been desperately trying to get across to him."[26]

Rechlessnesse goes on to argue that it is even less likely for learned men such as clerics to win salvation, as those that built Noah's ark (a typological symbol of the Church) were lost in the Deluge. To make this point, Rechlessnesse ironically confesses that he himself has tried the path of learning (although, as we see, not for the proper end):

Thus ich, Rechlessnesse, haue rad registres and bokes,
And fond ich neuere, in faith for to telle treuthe,
That Clergie of Cristes mouth comended was euere.   (XII. 274–276)[27]

His final conclusion, then, is that

Aren none rathere raueshed fro the ryghte by-leyue
Cominliche than clerkes most knowynge and connynge;
And none sonnere ysaued ne saddere in the by-leyue
Than plouhmen and pastours and poure comune peuple.   (XII. 290–293)

---

[25] A. H. Chroust, "Contribution to the Medieval Discussion: 'utrum Aristoteles sit salvatus,'" *Journal of the History of Ideas* 6 (1945): 231–238.

[26] Joseph S. Wittig, " 'Piers Plowman' Passus IX–XII: Elements in the Design of the Inward Journey," *Traditio* 28 (1972): 230.

[27] C. D. Benson, in "Augustinian Irony in *Piers Plowman,*" *Notes and Queries* 221 (1976): 51–54, has discovered another irony in Rechlessnesse's diatribe against learning. In XII.288 he quotes from Augustine's *Confessions,* "Ecce ipsi idioti rapiunt celum, vbi nos sapientes in inferno mergimur"; however, in context Augustine is not attacking learning but his own inability to put his learning to good advantage (53).

Again, we have two opposed extreme positions: Study and Scripture are zealous to guard knowledge from idle curiosity lest it be cheapened, while Rechlessnesse goes so far as to make learning an actual hindrance to salvation. As before, Ymaginatif provides the solution. And, as before, his views argue for a charitable God who would encourage, not punish, man's efforts to reach Truth:

Ne of Sortes, ne of Salamon no scripture can telle
Whether thei be in helle other in heuene; other Aristotle the wise.
Ac god is so good, ich hope sitthe he gaf hem wittes
To wissen ous weyes ther-with that wenen to be saued,
And the bettere for here bookes—to bidden we been holde
That god for hus grace gyue here saules reste;
For lettred men were but lewede men зut ne were the lore of tho clerkes. (XV. 193–199)

In addition, learning can keep a man from falling into wanhope, for "he that knoweth cleregie can sonnere a-ryse / Out of synne" (XV. 111–112).

Finally, a concern related to predestination also arises in Passus XII. Rechlessnesse lists several examples of surprising (at least to human logic) salvations. A thief who died with Jesus, Mary Magdalene who loved lechery, David who murdered to obtain another's wife, Paul who persecuted Christians—all received mercy. Therefore,

By that that Salamon seith hit semeth that no wyght
Wot ho is worthi for wele other for wicke,
Whether he is worthi to wele other to wickede pyne:
Sunt iusti atque sapientes, et opera eorum in manu dei sunt. (XII. 271–273)

This passage calls to mind the important controversy over grace and works. As Rechlessnesse sees it, grace is all. But in the next passus the Dreamer will be confronted by Trajan, whose works were sufficient for God to accede to Gregory's plea. At the moment, though, the Dreamer is concerned with the precedence of reward, as he indicates in his comments on the thief:

And for he by-knew on the crois and to Crist schrof hym,
He was sonnere ysaued than seynt Iohan the Baptist,
And er Adam other Ysaie other eny of the prophetes,
That hadden leye with Lucyfer meny longe зeres.
A robber was y-raunsoned rather than thei alle;
With-oute penaunce other passion other eny other peyne
He passede forth pacientliche to perpetuel blisse. (XII. 256–262)

Ymaginatif solves this dilemma as well, this time in a thoroughly orthodox (even "Dantean") way:

He [the thief] sit nother with seynt Iohan with Symon ne with Iude,
Ne with maydenes ne with martris ne with mylde wydewes,
Bote as a soleyn by hym-self and serued vp-on the grounde.

. . . .
Ryȝt as Traianus, the trewe knyght tulde nat deep in helle,
That oure lord ne hadde hym lyghtliche out so leyueth of the theef in heuene.
For he ys in the lowest heuene yf oure byleyue beo trewe. (XV. 143–145, 150–
152)

Although the position of the virtuous pagan is not explicitly discussed,
in light of the liberal attitude Ymaginatif has taken toward those who
faciunt quod in se est, we can infer that they, like the thief, probably hold a
lower place in heaven.

One other question runs throughout the poem and underlies all three
of the questions just discussed: the problem of grace vs. works. This
question directly involves the virtuous pagan, if a pagan's meritorious
works might justify his salvation. John McNamara concludes that

> Langland does not opt for one extreme pole or the other in the fourteenth century
> controversy between conservative Augustinians and radical Ockhamists. . . . The
> poem may perhaps be read as an extended dialectic in which various positions
> are allowed to present themselves and to oppose one another, with the hope that
> out of this opposition would come some resolution of the problem of grace and
> merit.[28]

While I agree that the poet refrains from adopting an extreme position,
in general his poem places more emphasis on the value of works. This is
evident as early as the pardon scene, when Piers learns that man shall be
rewarded according to his works: *"Qui bona egerunt ibunt in uitam eternam: /
Qui uero mala, in ignem eternum"* (X. 287). Hort calls the pardon "essentially
Pelagian" because "it is based on his confidence in the power of human
nature to do that which is good, and thus earn its own salvation."[29] The
Athanasian Creed from which the pardon is taken *verbatim* has itself been
identified with a semi-Pelagian environment, which explains its emphasis
on man's free will and responsibility for his acts.[30] This is evident even
in the phrase *"vult salvus esse"* in verses 1 and 28 of the Creed—a phrase
that reminds us of Will's words to Holychurche, "How ich may sauy my
saule" (II. 80). According to the "damnatory clauses" of the Creed, there

---

[28] McNamara 125.

[29] Hort 63. Langland may have omitted the tearing of the pardon in the C-text to clarify
his position on the importance of good works. Many critics of the B-text have seen Piers'
action as his realization that without grace, no amount of good effort can avail. As Lawlor
puts it (*"Piers Plowman:* The Pardon Reconsidered," *Modern Language Review* 45 [1950]: 452),
"We see now the measure not of England's corruption only, but the measure of man's best,
and its highest soul is infinitely short of Divine Goodness." McNamara agrees: "Any
prescription to do good works extracted from the Creed must also allow for the Creed's
insistence on grace" (95). Denise Baker goes so far as to see plowing and pilgrimage as
representing the views of the Nominalists (man can earn grace through good works) and
the Augustinians (grace is necessary to accomplish good works) respectively. Thus, "confronted with the obvious discrepancy between the words of Truth's document and the claim
that it is a pardon, Piers is forced to repudiate his previous Nominalist position. The reader,
shocked and bewildered by Piers' response, also comes to a realization of his own fallibility"
("From Plowing" 725).

[30] J.N.D. Kelly, *The Athanasian Creed* (London: Adam and Charles Black, 1964) 73, 119.

is only one avenue to salvation: "Quicunque vult salvus esse, ante omnia opus est ut teneat catholicam fidem" (verse 1); "Haec est fides catholica: quam nisi quis fideliter firmiterque crediderit, salvus esse non poterit" (verse 48).[31] The tenets of faith professed in the Creed concern the Trinity (verses 3–28) and the dual nature of Christ as equally God and man (verses 29–37). Both of these points are addressed in *Piers Plowman* (in Abraham's teachings on the Trinity, XIX. 212–242, and the Samaritan's elaboration in XX. 111–196, and in the image of Christ jousting in Piers' arms in XXI. 21). But these points of correct belief are overshadowed by the necessity of action; accordingly, Langland chose to quote from the Creed a clause relating to deeds, not doctrine.

In *Dowel*, the Dreamer gravitates to an extreme dependence on grace by seizing on baptism as a guarantee of salvation, by denying any value to learning, and by stressing predestination as beyond human logic, rendering man's attempts to do well futile. As we have seen, Ymaginatif's replies to all these charges emphasize the importance of works: baptism alone is not sufficient; learning put in the service of good is laudable; the notion of degrees of reward renders some of God's decisions less mystifying and indicates that man's actions *do* count. Most decisive, however, is the presentation of Trajan as a concrete example of the efficacy of good works, which makes doctrine pale by comparison (which explains Trajan's dramatic lines of entrance, " 'Ye, baw for bookes!' " in XIII. 74).[32] As mentioned above, Langland alters the legend to omit the possibility of baptism and minimizes the importance of Gregory's intercession, placing the focus squarely on Trajan's works. On the other hand, XVIII. 122–163 is an insert in the C-text which argues against this phenomenon; here, Liberum Arbitrium claims that Saracens may be saved, but only "yf thei so by-leyuede, / In the lengthynge of here lyf to leyue on holychurche" (XVIII. 123–124).[33]

Given the fact that Trajan insists he did *not* hold Christian beliefs (XIII. 77, 86), how can we reconcile his position with the statement about the Saracens' salvation? Liberum Arbitrium goes on to explain that Saracens may possess charity:

Hit is a kynde thyng, a creature hus creatour to honoure;
For ther is no man that mynde hath that ne meoketh hym and by-secheth
To that lord that hym lyf lente and lyflode him sendeth.   (XVIII. 153–155)

---

[31] Kelly 17, 20.

[32] See Wittig 258; McNamara 110–117; Frank 61–62; Adams 389–391.

[33] Examining the various manuscripts of the poem, Russell finds that several contain a variant reading, "in the lettynge of her lyf"; thus he correlates these lines to Uthred of Boldon's theory of the *clara visio* at the moment of death (110–112). Quite likely Langland was familiar with Uthred's views, but I find it hard to believe that we should read these lines as Russell argues. Would Langland have been content to introduce such an idea without elaboration? Even Russell concedes that "Nowhere else in the poem, in any of its versions, can I find similar propositions advanced" (112).

But the same *kynde* which inclines pagans to charity can also lead them astray: "And when kynde hath hus cours and no contrarye fyndeth, / Thenne is lawe lost and lewete vnknowen" (XVIII. 161–162).

The fact that these words come from Liberum Arbitrium reminds us of man's choice in this matter, though; he must not necessarily follow *kynde.* Ymaginatif argues for the hope of salvation for those pagans who "ne transuersed aȝens the lawe" (XV. 209), a feat admittedly difficult but apparently not beyond the scope of man's efforts.[34] And Trajan stands as the exemplar of a pagan who combined love *and* law, the necessary combination for salvation: "Loue, withoute leel by-leyue and my lawe ryghtful / Sauede me Sarrasyn soule and body bothe" (XIII. 86–87); later he adds, "For lawe with-oute leaute leye ther a bene!" (XIII. 92). (This echoes Holychurche's sentiment in II. 185, "Chastite with-oute charite worth cheynid in helle.") Thus salvation depends not so much on Christian belief as on the ability to operate under the Old and New Covenants of adhering to moral law and practicing charity.

None, however, would have enjoyed salvation without the introduction of the New Covenant, whose first effect was the Harrowing. Because of its importance in marking the turning point from the Old Law to the New, we can regard the Harrowing (Passus XXI) as the thematic climax of the poem.

With this in mind, let us turn directly to Passus XXI, in which the Harrowing occurs.[35] First, as in *St. Erkenwald,* the event of the Harrowing serves here to establish divine mastery of the universe. The medieval conception of the three-tiered universe is schematized in the first passus (the tower of truth, the field of folk, the castle of care), and the position of earth is subtly reinforced by the reference to "Myddelerd" when Fortune places Will before a mirror (XII. 170). The name of Jesus is recognized in heaven and on earth; however, the name "Christ" signifies his role as conqueror of Hell and thus master of the entire universe:

Myght no deth hym for-do ne adoun brynge,
That he ne aros and regnede and rauesshede helle;
And tho was he 'conquerour' called of quyke and of dede.   (XXII. 51–53)

---

[34] In this context, Wittig's observation that the poet chose to emphasize the *activity* of the imagination by his choice of the "-if" ending for Ymaginatif seems appropriate (270). Even the name of this character reminds us of the importance of action as opposed to the Dreamer's tendency toward spiritual inertia.

[35] This scene has received much critical attention; for example, Donald Wesling ("Eschatology and the Language of Satire in *Piers Plowman,*" *Criticism* 10 [1968]: 286) singles out the scene to illustrate structural irony in the poem, since it is juxtaposed with the two final anti-climactic passus. Lawlor (*Essay* 300–301) likewise recognizes the structural importance of the Harrowing, characterizing the poem as triangular rather than unilinear because of the peculiar nature of Dobet. In addition, others have recognized this scene as the poem's climax; see, for example, S. T. Knight, "Satire in *Piers Plowman,*" in *Piers Plowman: Critical Approaches,* ed. S.S. Hussey (London: Methuen and Co. Ltd., 1969) 303; Carruthers 139; and Bloomfield, *Apocalypse* 123–127.

Besides establishing God's reign in all levels of the universe—a spatial concept—the Harrowing in *Piers Plowman* is also (and primarily) used to establish a demarcation line in the continuum of time. It has long been recognized that the *Dowel, Dobet,* and *Dobest* sections deal essentially with different time periods; Henry W. Wells, who first delineated an organized pattern in the poem as opposed to a series of "social vignettes," pointed out that each of these sections is governed by one Person of the Trinity (the Father, Son, and Holy Ghost respectively).[36] Later, he took this association one step further to see the poem as (among other things) an historical allegory, with *Dowel* representing the pre-Christian world of the Father, *Dobet* the world during Christ's lifetime, and *Dobest* the world after the dispensation of the Holy Spirit.[37] (This historical progression may have been influenced by the ideas of Joachim of Flora, who divided temporality into three ages.[38]) At the same time, of course, we must keep in mind that the *Dowel* and *Dobest* sections deal ostensibly with fourteenth-century England—one minor example of how richly layered the poem is and why it resists any simple interpretation.

By concentrating on the Harrowing as the climax of the poem, we can better see the resulting divisions of time into three epochs, which are clearly characterized by the terms of the various legal documents which mark off these periods.[39] It is fitting here to note the poet's emphasis on legality.[40] Langland's God does not use his *potentia absoluta* to overturn the order of the universe but adheres scrupulously to the law. For example, in his confrontation with Lucifer before releasing Hell's prisoners, Christ asserts that He is merely claiming His due, although He admits that He used guile (adopting human guise, or "jousting in Pier's arms") to rebut

---

[36] Wells, "Construction" 12; Frank 16.

[37] Henry W. Wells, "The Philosophy of *Piers Plowman*," *PMLA* 53 (1938): 349.

[38] Bloomfield (*Apocalypse* 66) summarizes Joachim's theory as follows:

The period of the Old Testament was primarily the age of the Father; the period from the time of Jesus down to roughly Joachim's time was that of the Son; and the third age, which is a naturally completing period, should be that of the Holy Ghost, under whose aegis the Saracens and Jews would be converted and about which certain predictions could be made.

[39] Mary Carruthers ("Time, Apocalypse, and the Plot of *Piers Plowman*," in *Acts of Interpretation: The Text in Its Contexts, 700–1600: Essays on Medieval and Renaissance Literature in Honor of E. Talbot Donaldson* [Norman, Oklahoma: Pilgrim, 1982] 185) has also recognized the Harrowing in this regard but does not make the connection between the terms of the dispensation and the documents in *Piers Plowman*. She does mention, however, an interesting change in the grammatical texture of the poem which evidences the fundamental significance of the Harrowing. Through the Tree of Charity episode, sentences describing actions are joined by *and, ac,* and *thanne,* with an occasional *til.* Not until Passus 18, when Christ stands before the gates of Hell, do other constructions appear: *thus, so, for, but,* the subordinating conjunctions, and *but x . . . y,* or *siþen x . . . y.* "This is a perfect formal narrative expression of what Saint Paul writes in Col. 3.3–4. . . . Christ's triumph makes apparent the causes previously hidden" (183–184).

[40] See, for example, John A. Alford, "Literature and Law in Medieval England," *PMLA* 92 (1977): 941–951; William J. Birnes, "Christ as Advocate: The Legal Metaphor of *Piers Plowman*," *Annuale Mediaevale* 16 (1975): 71–93; Rudolf Kirk, "References to the Law in *Piers Plowman*," *PMLA* 48 (1932): 322–327; and Anna Baldwin, "The Double Duel in *Piers Plowman* B. XVIII and C. XXI," *Medium Aevum* 50 (1981): 64–78.

Lucifer's guile (appearing to Eve in the form of a serpent). His sacrifice is offered as payment for man's sins: "And al that man mys-dude ich, man, to amenden hit" (XXI. 392); thus He can say with assurance,

So leyf hit nat, Lucifer that ich aȝeyns the lawe
Fecche here eny synful soule souereynliche by maistrie;
Bot thorgh ryght and reson raunson here myne lige;
Non ueni soluere legem, sed adimplere.   (XXI. 396–398)[41]

A similar concern for legal form is shown in each epoch, characterized by a distinct "document."

My arrangement differs somewhat, however, from Wells': I would contend that the *Visio* deals primarily with an Old Testament outlook, based on the contractual nature of Piers' pardon, "*Qui bona egerunt ibunt in uitam eternam: / Qui vero mala, in ignem eternum*" (X. 287).[42] (At the same time, since the poem is circular, the *Visio* also relates to the Last Judgment.) As we have seen, the *Dowel* section represents the Dreamer's own intellectual efforts and does not enter the historical progression, which takes up again with *Dobet,* the period of Christ and the introduction of the New Covenant, "*Dilige deum et proximum tuum*" (XX. 13).[43] *Dobest* portrays an imminent Judgment; therefore, this period of time is marked by the warning "*redde quod debes*" (XXII. 187). Regarding the poem as a sequential movement through divine history reinforces the importance of the Harrowing: "As the speeches of Christ and the devils make clear, it is an event which both looks backward in time to redress the disjunction of man and God caused by the Fall, and looks forward to the end of time in the Last Judgment."[44]

Further, an examination of the *Visio* indicates that it can be used as a guide to sketch the broad outlines of each of these epochs. Piers first enters the poem as a guide to Truth; he is detained to plow his half-acre; then he receives his pardon from Truth. It is significant that although at first he planned to seek Truth (via an allegorical road dotted with signposts

---

[41] Pearsall (332–333, n. 299) elaborates on the legalities of the scene, noting that by Langland's time the theory of "devil's rights" was old-fashioned theologically.

[42] Pearsall (174, n. 291, and 58, n. 78a) suggests that the legality of the pardon would have been familiar to the poet's audience through the "Charter of Christ," in which the "deed" of redemption is written on the parchment of Christ's skin, with the ink of his blood.

[43] The legality of this document is obvious because it is "letters patent"—"an open letter, as from the sovereign, for all to see, recording some agreement or contract" (Pearsall 306, n. 7).

[44] Carruthers, *Search* 142. Other progressions in the poem have been noted. Ben H. Smith, *Traditional Imagery of Charity in Piers Plowman* (Hague: Mouton, 1966), argues that the poem advances from natural law to scriptural law to a period of grace (84–85). Barbara Raw, "Piers and the Image of God in Man," in *Piers Plowman: Critical Approaches,* ed. S.S. Hussey (London: Methuen and Co. Ltd., 1969) sees the poem as a gradual restoration of the image of God in mankind (154–155). In the same way, Elizabeth Kirk (179–180) sees the poem as three confrontations between man's will and God's. John F. Adams, "*Piers Plowman* and the Three Ages of Man," *Journal of English and Germanic Philology* 61 (1962): 23–41, traces in the poem the progressive difficulties, moral and spiritual, each man faces.

of the Ten Commandments), at last *Truth* sends a message to *him*. This, in miniature, details the historical progression of the entire poem and helps explain the significance of each document. Piers first directs the repentant folk to seek Truth (God) through the Ten Commandments, issued in the eye-for-an-eye spirit of the Old Testament. But first, the plowing of the half-acre (in other words, the spiritual cultivation of "Myddelerd") takes place, an action which corresponds to *Dobet* or the Christian dispensation. Finally, through Piers Truth (God) sends His pardon, actually the terms of Judgment.[45] This portion of the *Visio* corresponds to *Dobest,* which does not actually depict the Judgment but leads up to it. At last, then, Truth finds all men.

Let us now examine each of the documents and their corresponding epochs in more detail. The scene which has provoked the greatest amount of attention occurs in Passus X, when Piers receives the first of these documents, a "pardon" from Truth. In the B-text—the one usually selected for discussion of this passus because of its greater dramatic value— Piers reads the pardon, hears the priest's disparagement of it, and then tears the pardon in "pure tene" (B. VII. 116). This unexpected action has produced several conjectures: that the pardon is invalid,[46] that this pardon is valid but the action symbolizes a general rejection of paper pardons from Rome,[47] that the pardon actually becomes a pardon only when Piers rips it,[48] that Piers is angry at the priest and tears the pardon as he abandons the Active Life,[49] that Piers acknowledges the impossibility of meeting the pardon's terms.[50] Critics have also pointed out that Piers' action is reminiscent of Moses' breaking the stone tablets on his return from Sinai; in each instance, the principal character is angry at an unworthy priest and vents his rage on the nearest object.[51] Common exegetical tradition

---

[45] Vasta mentions that Piers oscillates between the individual soul and the Church; when he receives the pardon at the end of the *Visio,* he symbolizes the Church, the intermediary between God and man (133). Katherine Trower, "The Figure of Hunger in *Piers Plowman,*" *American Benedictine Review* 24 (1973), also sees Piers' actions in the *Visio* as earning a period of grace for the folk (256).

[46] Frank provides a convenient summary of those critics who feel the pardon is invalid (25, n. 7). Susan McLeod also gives an excellent review of criticism on the pardon scene in "The Tearing of the Pardon in *Piers Plowman,*" *Philological Quarterly* 56 (1977): 14–17.

[47] John Burrow, "The Action of Langland's Second Vision," in *Style and Symbolism in Piers Plowman,* ed. Robert J. Blanch (Knoxville, Tenn.: University of Tennessee Press, 1969) 223; J.V. Holleran, "The Role of the Dreamer in *Piers Plowman,*" *Annuale Mediaevale* 7 (1966): 36; Frank 28. Wittig expands upon this view, claiming that the pardon scene is meant to exclude "the whole attitude toward *bona spiritualia* for which the buying and selling of pardons is an emblem" (277).

[48] Rosemary Woolf, "The Tearing of the Pardon," in *Piers Plowman: Critical Approaches,* ed. S.S. Hussey (London: Methuen and Co. Ltd., 1969) 70.

[49] John Lawlor, "*Piers Plowman:* The Pardon Reconsidered," *Modern Language Review* 45 (1950), 455; Donaldson 162–163; Meroney 18; Carruthers, *Search* 71–72.

[50] Lawlor, *Essay* 282–283; Raw 164.

[51] Mary (Carruthers) Schroeder, "The Tearing of the Pardon," *Philological Quarterly* 49 (1970): 10–11; Meroney 18.

interpreted this as a type of the change from Old Law to New.[52] Another analogue exists in the tearing of the Temple veil, also symbolizing the change from the Old Covenant to the New.[53]

In the C-text, however, this scene is considerably scaled down. Piers does not tear the pardon; instead, the Dreamer merely tells us that he awoke when "the preest thus and Perkyn of the pardon Iangled" (X. 292). The omission of the dramatic action of B allows us to focus on the message of the pardon. The text itself, *"Qui bona egerunt ibunt in uitam eternam: / Qui vero mala, in ignem eternum,"* would have been recognized by the poet's audience as coming from the Athanasian Creed.[54] In this context, the lines clearly refer to the Last Judgment:

qui passus est pro salute nostra, descendit ad inferna, resurrexit a mortuis, ascendit ad caelos, sedet ad dexteram Patris: inde uenturus iudicare uiuos et mortuos, ad cuius aduentum omnes homines resurgere habent cum corporibus suis et reddituri sunt de factis propriis rationem. Et qui bona egerunt ibunt in uitam eternam, qui uero mala in ignem aeternum.

Haec est fides catholica quam nisi quisque fideliter firmiterque crediderit, saluus esse non poterit.

(Who suffered for our salvation, descended into Hell, rose again from the dead, ascended into heaven, sitteth at the right hand of the Father, from whence He shall come to judge the quick and the dead. At whose coming all men shall rise again with their bodies and shall give account for their own works. And they who have done good shall go into life eternal, and they who indeed *have done* evil into eternal fire.

This is the Catholic Faith, which except a man shall have believed faithfully and firmly he cannot be in a state of salvation.[55])

This is, indeed, no pardon as it stands. However, the last line of this verse ("Qui bona egerunt . . .") would, to a medieval audience, quite likely have suggested its opening lines: the outline of the Passion, Harrowing, Resurrection, and Ascension. This is a pardon, then, but in the time scheme

---

[52] See, for example, Rabanus Maurus (*Commentaria in Exodum, P.L.,* Vol. 108, col. 224D):
Iratus quidem Moyses videtur tabulas testimonii digito Dei scriptas, collisisse atque fregisse: magno tamen mysterio figurata est iteratio testamenti, quoniam vetus fuerat abolendum, et constituendum novum.

[53] Lawlor, "Pardon" 456.

[54] The Athanasian Creed was regularly used during the service of Prime, and "the whole service of Matins, including Lauds, Prime, and Terce, was most popular in England as a preparation for the Mass" (A. E. Burn, "Creeds," in *Encyclopaedia of Religion and Ethics,* 1913 ed.) Kelly confirms that during the Middle Ages the general practice was weekly recitation of the Creed on Sundays at Prime (44). Pearsall, however, states that the Creed was recited on some special feast-days in place of the Apostles' Creed (141, n. 236). In any case, the lines would have been known to a fourteenth-century audience.

[55] A.E. Burn, *An Introduction to the Creeds and to the Te Deum* (London: Methuen and Co., 1899), 193 (Latin text) and 197 (English translation). D. A. Lawton ("*Piers Plowman:* On Tearing— and Not Tearing—the Pardon," *Philological Quarterly* 60 [1981]: 420) points out that if we visualize the B-text action so that Piers tears the pardon horizontally in two, he has literally divided "the sheep from the goats" in a forecast of the Judgment.

of the poem Christ's sacrifice has not yet taken place. We are reminded of this by the *Visio*'s overall emphasis on the First Member of the Trinity, indicating an underlying Old Testament frame.[56] In addition, the action involving Piers' half-acre reflects a primitive time, when men could be controlled only by their most basic urge, hunger.[57] The one court scene we are shown depicts an Old Testament ethic. Wrong must be punished, even if Pees, the injured party, wishes mercy, not strict justice, for his foe. The allegorical characters which figure importantly, Conscience and Reason, are those we would expect to predominate in an Old Testament setting, while Mede, a dangerously ambivalent character, represents an evil which has always existed in opposition to the church. (Even Cain's murder of his brother sprang from an offering of mede to God.) The Seven Deadly Sins also make their appearance, although, surprisingly enough, they do so to confess. Repentance, who hears their confessions, prays for mercy in a speech which recounts the events of Christ's life and His holy mission of saving the sinful. But, within the constraints of this Old Testament setting, no forgiveness is forthcoming. The best that can occur is Hope's blast upon a horn, gathering the folk together to seek Truth (VIII. 152–157).[58] And when Piers offers to tell them the way, even he admits his limitations; he has learned the way to Truth not through any specific divine revelation but through Conscience and Kyndewit[59]— and forty years of following Truth.[60] Although his directions to Truth delineate the way of the Ten Commandments, he warns the folk that Grace and Charity must also be approached (VIII. 254–259). If we identify Truth as God the Father, Charity as Christ, and Grace as the Holy Spirit, we see that no one member of the Trinity can be reached in isolation. Thus, despite Piers' assurance that all are kin to Mercy at Truth's court, the people realize that they need a guide to find their way. But first they

---

[56] Carruthers (*Search* 73) and Kirk (92–93) point out that the *Visio* represents the Old Testament not in any true historical sense but in Piers' psychological state, his contractual conception of religion. As Carruthers puts it, "Any fourteenth-century man who tries to live simply according to law and justice without the sustaining power of grace is a moral type of the ancient Hebrews under the Old Law who also lacked grace" (73). Donaldson further suggests that Piers may, in the anagogical sense, stand for the prophets who waited patiently for the coming of Christ—as on the moral level patience precedes charity (180).

[57] Schroeder 13.

[58] According to Pearsall (136, n. 152), the horn is the trumpet of salvation mentioned in the *Exsultet* for Holy Saturday celebrating the Resurrection. Since the Resurrection has not yet occurred in the poem's time scheme, it is appropriate that *Hope* blows the horn.

[59] See also Randolph Quirk, "Langland's Use of Kynde Wit and Inwit," *Journal of English and Germanic Philology* 52 (1953): 182–185.

[60] Forty commonly represents a probationary period, a time of trial and testing; for example, the 40-day Deluge (Genesis 7:4), the Israelites' 40 years of wandering (Numbers 32:13), the 40-day period of fasting undergone by Moses, Elias, and Christ (Exodus 32:28, 3 Kings 19:8, Matthew 4:2). Katherine Trower ("Temporal Tensions in the *Visio* of *Piers Plowman*," *Mediaeval Studies* 35 [1973]: 397) believes that the number 40 prefigures the trials Piers will undergo with the folk in plowing the half-acre. However, Piers has already served his 40 years, which makes him eligible to guide the others and to receive Truth's pardon—a pardon which indicates, by its connotations of Judgment, that the time of testing must end.

agree to help Piers sow his half-acre—an episode which illustrates their need for Truth as Piers struggles to put them to work.

At the end of Passus IX, just before Piers receives his pardon from Truth in the opening of the next passus, we encounter an apocalyptic passage:

Thorwe flodes and foule wederes frutes shullen faile,
Pruyde and pestilences shal muche puple fecche.
Thre shupes and a shaft with an vm. folwyng,
Shal brynge bane and bataile on bothe half the mone.
And thanne shal deth with-drawe and derthe be Iustice,
And Dawe the deluere deye for defaute,
Bote god of hus goodnesse graunte ous a trewe.   (XI. 349–355)

Although Skeat interprets this as a mock prophecy satirizing contemporary doom-sayers,[61] this description can be taken as a prophecy of the signs portending the Last Judgment. As such, we see that in the next passus God does "graunte a trewe" through Truth, who purchases a pardon for Piers and his fellow workers. (The word "purchase," of course, calls to mind the ransom of Christ.)

As we have seen, the actual pardon is implicit; the words which Piers, the priest, and the Dreamer read portray only the harsh terms of the Last Judgment. If we keep an Old Testament setting in mind, it comes as no surprise then that the Dreamer soon awakens "meteles and moneyles" (X. 295)—Christ has not yet come to offer His body (eucharistically, "mete") as a ransom to purchase mankind.

It may seem that the poet is having it all ways in the *Visio*—there are undoubtedly contemporary references, the entire Christian story is briefly told, and yet the theological emphasis definitely falls within an Old Testament context, symbolized best by the legalistic terms of the pardon. At the same time, the pardon is introduced by an apocalyptic prophecy, and its place in the Athanasian Creed bespeaks Judgment. All of this is possible because of the nature of Scripture, the elemental belief that the Old Testament is fulfilled by the New. This allows the poet to draw upon all epochs while simultaneously maintaining a predominant Old Testament orientation. The pardon itself, the climax of the *Visio*, emphasizes the close connection between Old Testament justice and the justice which will be displayed at the Last Judgment. Between these two eras lies man's only real hope for escaping that justice—the Christian dispensation. Without mercy, the folk cannot enter the gate to Truth; likewise, the Church believed that none who died before Christ could enter heaven. (Piers makes this clear in his directions to Truth's court in VIII. 288–291: "Mercy is a mayde there hath myght ouer hem alle; / And hue is sybbe to alle synful and hure sone bothe. / And thorwe the help of hem two hope thow non other, / Thow myght gete grace ther so thow go by tyme.")

---

[61] See Skeat's notes on Passus IX. 349–355.

The most they could hope for was a resting-place in Abraham's bosom, usually figured as the upper portion of Hell.

Appropriately, then, the next epoch the poem deals with achieves its climax in Hell. (I realize that by making this jump I ignore almost all of *Dowel.* As noted before, Passus XI through XVII do not enter into the historical progression of the poem but deal with a psychological progression as the Dreamer tries to attain an intellectual grasp of his faith.) After a long period of scholastic questioning over various matters—some of which we have already examined—the Dreamer in Passus XVII at last turns his attention to charity (ll. 284–285), the subject which then occupies the *Dobet* section of the poem.[62]

In Passus XIX, Liberum Arbitrium responds to the Dreamer's request, "telle and teche me to Charite" (l. 2) by leading him to the tree of Ymagodei. The conjunction of free will, tree, and image of God (in which man was made) immediately calls to mind the fate of Adam and Eve. But the allegory is more complex. We see the results of the Fall for their heirs; as Elde shakes the tree, the devil lurks nearby to catch the "fruit":

> ... the deuel was wel redy,
> And gederide hem all to-gederis bothe grete and smale,
> Adam and Abraham and Ysaye the prophete,
> Sampson and Samuel and seynt Iohan the baptist,
> And bar hem forth baldely no body tho hym lette,
> And made of holy men hus horde in *limbo inferni,*
> Ther is derknesse and drede and the deuel maister.   (XIX. 111–117)

As a result of this situation—which obtained up to the time of John the Baptist, traditionally Christ's forerunner even in Hell—another Master had to be established in Hell.[63] In terms of the poem's imagery, we learn "That Iesus sholde Iuste ther-fore in Iugement of armes, / Who sholde fecche this frut the feend other Iesus self" (XIX. 129–130).[64] But the Dreamer, after seeing a quick succession of scenes from Christ's life, wakes

---

[62] Donaldson 180 and Vasta 125. See Britton J. Harwood's discussion of this scene in "*Liberum Arbitrium* in the C-Text of *Piers Plowman,*" *Philological Quarterly* 52 (1973): 680–695. He concludes that Liberum Arbitrium's failure provides "the vacuum into which God's love advances" (695).

[63] Smith points out that the tree of Christ probably can be affiliated with the tree of Jesse, used to join matter traditionally connected with the old dispensation to matter traditionally connected with the new (62). This supports the concept of the poem as an historical allegory, moving from the Old Testament epoch to the Incarnation, which takes place within the context of the tree of charity, when "*Libera-Uoluntas-Dei* lauhte the myddel shoriere, / And hitte after the fende . . . / *Filius,* by the faders wil flegh with *Spiritus Sanctus,* / To ransake that rageman and reue hym hus apples" (XIX. 119–122). Trower also relates the Tree of Charity to two parables of fig trees from the New Testament ("Hunger" 243–256).

[64] The jousting imagery used throughout in relation to Christ's sacrifice corresponds with the cycle plays, in which the soldiers make a game of nailing Christ to the cross as a knight mounting his horse. See Wilbur Gaffney, "The Allegory of the Christ-Knight in *Piers Plowman,*" *PMLA* 46 (1931): 155–168, who postulates a possible source for the treatment of Christ as knight in *Piers Plowman* and cites relevant passages for comparison in the Towneley and York plays.

before the "jousting" takes place, on "Mydlentens Soneday" (XIX. 183).
Since Lent corresponds to the pre-Christian era, we are not surprised
when the Dreamer meets Abraham, or Faith, who teaches him of the
Trinity.[65] Abraham has another lesson to impart as well, one which harks
back to Piers' pardon. Piers had received a pardon "for hym and for hus
heyres for euere to be asoiled" (X. 4); likewise, Abraham received a
pardon:

For hym-self seide ich sholde haue and myn issue bothe
Lond and lordshup ynow and lyf with-outen ende.
To me and to myn issue more he by-hihte,
Mercy for oure mysdedes as meny tymes
As we wilnede and wolde with mouth and herte asken.   (XIX. 257–261)

The terms of each pardon are substantially the same, but neither pardon
is yet in effect, as the Dreamer sees when he looks into Abraham's lap:
"And ich loked in hus lappe a lazar lay ther-ynne, / With patriarkes
and prophetes pleiynge to-gederes" (XIX. 273–274). This is, of course,
Langland's version of Abraham's bosom (cf. Luke 16:22), whose inhabitants are the literal equivalents of the "fruit" gathered by the devil. As
Abraham informs the Dreamer, they must await Christ, "That shal de-
lyuery ous som day out of the deueles powere" (XIX. 284).[66] Thus both
pardons are valid; they merely remain ineffectual until sealed by Christ's
sacrifice.

Earlier we observed that in Passus VIII, after the confession of the Seven
Deadly Sins, no forgiveness was forthcoming—but Hope blew upon his
horn. In Passus XX, immediately after we learn that those in Abraham's
lap have not received mercy (" 'Alas!' ich seide, 'that synne so longe shal
lette / The myght of godes mercy that myghte ous alle amende!' " XIX.
288–289), Spes, or Hope, appears again. Spes can also be identified with
Moses, for he seeks a knight "That tooke me a maundement vp-on the
mounte of Synay" (XX.2). This reinforces the conjunction of the Old
and New Covenants, for in the rigid law of the Ten Commandments there
was also Hope—in the projected coming of Christ. With the Incarnation,
a new law was instituted, one which did not void the Decalogue but
imparted spirit to its letter: "Dilige deum et proximum tuum." These words,
clearly identified with Christ and the way of love, rather than justice,

[65] Ames states that "It was during Lent, as the Church relived each year the events leading
up to the Crucifixion, that the account of Abraham in Genesis was read in missal and
breviary, the marginal note in the breviary reading 'Abraham de Trinitate.' That Langland
was following the liturgical pattern in his recreation of the Passion is clear from the fact
that the dreamer meets Abraham on mid-Lent Sunday. In the scheme of the poem, Lent
represents the time in the history of the world of the long centuries of Old Testament
preparation for Christ" (87).
[66] In the B version, the Samaritan cares for the injured man and then "in his lappe hym
layde" (XVII. 70). Smith points out that this contrasts effectively with the description of
Abraham's lap in B. XVI. 255–269. "The contrast is the more effective because it is only
Christ, typified in the Good Samaritan, who can free those in Abraham's lap from Satan's
power" (80).

constitute the letter Hope carries. The Dreamer, who does not understand the relationship between the teachings of Abraham on the Trinity and Hope's letter, is now in the same position as the priest in Passus X who did not comprehend Piers' pardon. Piers and the priest "iangled"; Abraham, Spes, and Will "wente in the way thus wordyng of this matere" (XX. 46).

One nice touch is that the poet specifies that Hope's letter is written in Latin and Hebrew (XX. 4), emphasizing the fact that this letter applies to both New Covenant and Old, respectively.[67] Piers' pardon, with its connotations of the Second Coming, was written in Latin alone, for at last it would apply only to Christians, those who came after the Harrowing. Their predecessors had been judged accordingly and sentenced either to the torments of Hell or to the limbo of Abraham's bosom. In addition, Hope's letter is unsealed, awaiting the Harrowing:

'Nay,' he seyde, 'ich seke hym that hath the seel to kepe,
The whiche is Criste and Cristendome and a croys ther-on to honge.
Were hit ther-with a-seeled ich wote wel the sothe,
That Lucifers lordshup ligge sholde ful lowe.' (XX. 7–10)

When the Samaritan enters the scene, we know that the *plenitudo temporis* for the Incarnation has come: Faith and Hope could not heal the injured man if they would, but the Samaritan can. (This reminds us that in XIX. 138, Liberum Arbitrium taught Jesus "leche-crafte.") Traditionally, the parable of the Good Samaritan represented Christ's rescuing of mankind, so this makes a fitting preface to the actual scene in Hell. But in the poem itself the victory against Satan has not yet been won—a point subtly made when the Samaritan leads his charge to *lauacrum lex-dei* ("the bath of the law of God," or the baptismal font), located six or seven miles beside the new market (XX. 71–72). If Christ's mission in Hell is unsuccessful, *lauacrum lex-dei* can be located six miles from the "new market"— perhaps a fanciful indication of the New Covenant[68]—for in medieval numerology the number six represented the six ages of earth, or the extent of human limitations. (An interesting speculation here, although it may stretch the point too far, is that Truth may have "purchased" Piers' pardon at this "newe markett.") On the other hand, if Christ *is* successful, *lauacrum lex-dei* will be seven miles from the market, for seven is the number of fulfillment.[69]

---

[67] In the B-text, this is made clear by Anima's statement in XV. 574, "*Dilige deum et proximum is parfit Iewen lawe.*" In C. XX. 15 we are given a brief gloss on Spes' letter, "*In his duobus mandatis pendet tota lex et prophete,*" Christ's words in Matthew 22:40 which make clear the connection between the Old and New Covenants.

[68] Pearsall sees the new market as symbolizing "the busy world of getting and spending, the world of the Prologue, from which the life of the Christian must be momentarily detached" (309, n. 72).

[69] See, for example, Augustine's *Letter* LV, 9, 17 (in which the creation of the world in six days is seen as a token of six earthly ages) and his *Reply to Faustus*, XII, 8, in which the seventh day is characterized as the rest of the saints. Both the sixth and seventh days will

From the parable, the poem begins to move to the literal description of Jesus' battle with the devil. Faith explains what will happen, again establishing his Old Testament orientation by quoting Hosea 13:14, which was used as the key proof text for the Harrowing[70]:

> . . . with-inne thre dayes
> To walke and fecche fro the feonde Peers frut the Plouhman,
> And legge hit ther hym lyketh and Lucifer bynde,
> And forbete and bringe adoun bale and deth for euere;
> *O mors, ero mors tua!*
>
> (XXI. 31–34)

Witnessing the Passion, Faith curses the Jews for their 'vilanye' and prophesies their doom (XXI. 100–114). This is a response suitable to the Old Covenant, a cry for revenge. But in a master-stroke of dramatic irony, we see the inadequacy of his vituperative response. The Dreamer "drow in that deorknesse to *descendit ad inferna*" (XXI. 116)—the phrase from the Creed which marks the turning-point from justice to mercy—and witnesses the reconciliation of the Four Daughters of God.[71] Treuthe and Ryghtwisnesse, like Abraham, expect justice. Thus Treuthe contends that "The thyng that ones was in helle out cometh hit neuere" (XXI. 152), and Ryghtwisnesse adds, "For-thi let hem chewe as they chose" (XXI. 207). But Mercy and Peace, like the Samaritan, follow the new law of love.[72] The Harrowing portends a different era, as Pees suggests: "And Christ hath conuerted the kynde of ryghtwisnesse / In-to pees and pyte of hus pure grace" (XXI. 190–191). (We should also recall that Mercy is the sister whom Piers suggested the folk call upon; her hope for the souls' liberation from Hell justifies this.) The sisters' dispute is followed by Book's speech, which also predicts Jesus' victory; otherwise, "ich, Book, wole beo brent bote he arise to lyue" (XXI. 266)—in other words, Scripture must be fulfilled or burned.

At last, after so much elaborate preparation, we are shown Jesus standing outside Hell. The account corresponds closely to that given in the Gospel of Nicodemus (even in that Satan and Lucifer are two separate characters)[73] and, as already noted, great emphasis is put on the legality of the Harrowing, which fulfills the Old Testament laws rather than nullifying them:

---

culminate in the Judgment and Eternal Regeneration of the eighth (a number which is absent in this passage because it deals with Christ's mercy, the intermediate stage before Judgment).

[70] Pearsall notes that liturgically Hosea 13:14 was sung as an antiphon on Holy Saturday (321, n. 34a).

[71] For a full treatment of this motif, see Hope Traver, *The Four Daughters of God*, Bryn Mawr College Monographs, Monograph Series 6 (Philadelphia, 1907) 147–152, for *Piers Plowman;* 164–165 for a discussion of the scene's placement.

[72] In addition, Holleran notes that the reconciliation between the Daughters is like that between Abraham and Spes; Christ resolves the Daughters' problem as the Samaritan resolved the Dreamer's (49).

[73] Pearsall notes that this is an exegetical tradition established by Jerome (331, n. 274).

Dentem pro dente, et oculum pro oculo.
So lyf shal lyf lete ther lyf hath lyf anyented,
So that lyf quyte lyf the olde lawe hit asketh.   (XXI. 388–390)

Thus the Harrowing can be justified as the climax of *Piers Plowman* in terms of its thematic use. To this point in the poem, everything related to the historical allegory has looked forward to this great division in divine history; the Harrowing makes Piers' pardon effectual, since men now have grace to do well, and it seals Spes' letter. Furthermore, no other action in the poem is so richly overlaid with allegory and imagery: the Good Samaritan, or Charity, heals the injured man that Faith and Hope cannot even stop to look at; the Four Daughters of God are reconciled; Jesus jousts with the devil for Piers' fruit; Jesus claims His lawful rights over Hell and the souls imprisoned there.

To some critics, Christ's speech in Hell carries Origenistic tones of universal salvation, not only during the Harrowing (" 'Lo, me her,' quath oure lorde 'lyf and soule bothe, / For alle synful soules to saue oure beyere right.' " XXI. 373–374), but also in the next Judgment:

'May no pyement ne pomade ne presiouse drynkes
Moyste me to the fulle ne my thurst slake,
Til the vendage valle in the vale of Iosaphat,
And drynk ryght rype most *resurreccio mortuorum.*
Then shal ich come as a kyng with coroune and with angeles,
And haue out of helle alle menne soules.'   (XXI. 412–417)[74]

Because of his kinship with man, Christ will claim his legal right to exercise mercy:

'Ac to beo merciable to man thenne my kynde asketh;
....
For ich were an vnkynde kynge bote ich my kyn holpe,
And namelich at such a neode that neodes help asketh.' (XXI. 420, 443–444)[75]

However, Christ does not lead forth all the souls in Hell during the Harrowing; the poet maintains an orthodox stand by having Christ specify

---

[74] Chambers, for example, sees a tendency toward universal salvation in the poem (*Mind* 158); W. O. Evans ("Charity," in *Piers Plowman: Critical Approaches,* ed. S.S. Hussey [London: Methuen and Co., Ltd., 1969] 277) states that "The poem as a whole would seem to reveal the mind of a man whose inclinations lead him toward Origenism. But he is unsure and tends to draw back from the directly heretical statement." Hort also sees a modified version of universal salvation; Christ has given grace to all men, by which they are able to pay their debt and thus gain salvation (126). George Kane (*Middle English Literature: A Critical Study of the Romances, the Religious Lyrics, Piers Plowman* [London: Methuen and Co., Ltd., 1951] 196) asserts, "The striking thing was to find that in his mind there existed side by side with the sternness a deep and gentle tenderness embracing the whole of nature and even erring mankind, so long as misfortune, or the will to amend, or even ignorance excused its unregenerate state."

[75] Pearsall points out that the theology of these passages is not entirely heterodox, especially when compared with a work such as the *Prick of Conscience* (338–339, n. 420 and n. 430).

those to be released: " 'Thus by lawe,' quath oure lord 'lede ich wol fro hennes / Alle that ich louye and leyuede in my comynge' " (XXI. 445–446). This criterion would seem to include the patriarchs and prophets, a stock phrase used often in the poem (as, for example, in VIII. 88, X. 12, XII. 151), but it leaves ambiguous the fate of the non-Jewish pagans. Nevertheless, the fact that some souls are left behind is made clear; the fiends "dorst nat loken on oure lorde the leste of hem alle, / Bot leten hym leden forth which hym luste and leue whiche hym lykede" (XXI. 450–451). This lessens the likelihood of universal salvation at the Last Judgment as well, although admittedly this remains ambiguous:

'And ich, that am kynge ouer kynges shal come suche a tyme,
Ther that dom to the deoth dampneth alle wyckede;
And yf lawe wol ich loke on hem hit lyth in my grace,
Whether thei deye other deye nat dude thei neuere so ille.'   (XXI. 429–432)

This passage is an acknowledgment of the divine *potentia absoluta,* but it is modified by the conservative phrase "yf lawe wol," a reminder that Christ scrupulously adheres to legal bounds.

As the climactic vision of the Harrowing ends and the Four Daughters of God kiss and dance joyfully, the Dreamer awakes on Easter morning eager "To huyre holliche the masse and be housled after" (XXII. 3). Because communion was commonly given only on Easter during the fourteenth century, this is an especially appropriate response to the visions of *Dobet.*[76] The Dreamer, unlike those earlier in the poem who futilely sought repentance, has assurance of forgiveness now that the Passion and Harrowing have occurred. His participation in communion will indicate his membership in the Church Militant, with which *Dobest,* beginning with this passus, is concerned.

In addition, this makes a smooth transition from the Harrowing, for in Passus VIII Repentance described the descent into Hell in eucharistic terms: "A-bowte midday whanne most lyght ys and meeltyme of seyntes; / Feddest tho with this fresshe blod oure for-fadres in helle" (VIII. 133–134).[77] Thus the Dreamer's partaking of communion links him

---

[76] See, however, XXII. 387–392, which indicates that Langland either advocated or participated in a more regular communion. The latter possibility may indicate a clerical vocation. The Easter communion would still be of special significance, though, as it is even today. Furthermore, Easter communion was preceded by an annual penance, as decreed by the Fourth Lateran Council; and the sacrament was regarded as a cleansing of the soul through the infusion of the *habitus* of charity. See Yngve Brilioth, *Eucharistic Faith and Practice Evangelical and Catholic,* trans. A. G. Hebert (London: Society for Promoting Christian Knowledge, 1930) 91–93.

[77] This reference may allude to the legend found in *St. Patrick's Purgatory* that those who have passed through purgatory and wait in the earthly paradise for their summons to heaven are fed once a day by a light shining from heaven (*The South English Legendary,* ed. Carl Horstmann, EETS 87 [London: N. Trübner and Co., 1887] 216–217). This source was first noted by Mabel Day, " 'Mele Tyme of Seintes,' *Piers Plowman,* B, V, 500," *Modern Language Review* 27 (1932): 317–318. Pearsall notes the associated image of Christ as pelican, feeding His offspring with His own flesh and blood (135, n. 134) and the frequent representation of sinners as drinking blood from the wound in Christ's side (213, n. 54).

to those liberated from Hell in the first Harrowing and to those saved from Hell at the Judgment by their belief in Christ and allegiance to the Church.

We have seen that the *Visio* is characterized by the harshly legalistic pardon Piers received (*"Qui bona egerunt ibunt in uitam eternam: / Qui uero mala, in ignem eternum"*); *Dobet* can be associated with Spes' letter, sealed by Christ's crucifixion (*"Dilige deum et proximum tuum"*); the last section, *Dobest,* is marked by a repeated imperative which serves as a warning that the time of charity is drawing to an end: *redde quod debes* ("render what you owe"). The phrase is first introduced during Conscience's recapitulation of Jesus' life:

And [Christ] ȝaf Peers power and pardon he grauntede
To alle manere of men mercy and forȝyuenesse,
and ȝaf hym myghte to asoyle men of alle manere synnes,
In couenant that thei come and kneweliched to paye
To Peers pardon the Plouhman *redde quod debes.*

. . . .

A-non after an hyh vp in-to heuene
He wente, and woneth there and wol come atte laste,
And rewardy him right wel that *reddit quod debet,*
Payeth now parfitliche as pure treuthe wold.   (XXII. 183–187, 191–194)

Although *redde quod debes*—making restitution—does constitute the first step of penance, its significance seems much greater here.[78] If one follows *redde quod debes,* one can claim protection under Piers' pardon, and one can rest assured of reward at the Last Judgment. Like the first pardon given to Piers, *redde quod debes,* although not actually a written document, implies a legalistic sense, the necessity of fulfilling a contract to receive one's due. In a Christian context, it seems clear that as Christ fulfilled the law by offering His life for that of mankind, now Christians owe Christ the offering of themselves to the Church. As He exemplified charity, so should His followers. And this is precisely what *Dobest* inversely outlines—the failure of men to render charity to each other. The brewer cheats his customers; the curator exposes the corruption of the Pope and other high church officials; the lord and the king take more than their due from their subordinates (XXII. 398–481). As Conscience attempts to pull Christians together into Unity, or Holy Church, Antichrist attacks from without while their defenses are weakened from corruption within.

Many similarities exist between the *Visio* and the last two passus, but what was merely an agricultural scene early in the poem (Piers plowing

---

[78] As Pearsall puts it, "Restitution is not to be understood solely or primarily in material terms: it is, in a larger sense, the rendering of the debt of love to God and one's neighbour" (349, n. 187). Margaret Goldsmith (*The Figure of Piers Plowman: The Image on the Coin* [Cambridge: D. S. Brewer, 1981] 78) also mentions the larger meaning of *redde quod debes* as the offering of one's soul to God: "Langland's purpose is to make his contemporaries realise what a paltry substitute offering is Meed's money, when given for mass-pence or for a new church window."

his half-acre) has assumed scriptural significance: now Piers plows with four oxen that represent the Gospels and four bullocks that represent the Latin Fathers, sowing grains of cardinal virtues, with the harvest to be stored in Unity.[79] The food which was apparently literal in the *Visio* is here holy, "bred yblessid and godes body ther-vnder" (XXII. 387). In other words, the promise of the Old Testament has been fulfilled; and, with the mention of Antichrist, we become aware that the end of time is near.[80] Although Langland does not depict the Second Coming, the circular nature of the poem reminds us of Piers' pardon and its terms of judgment: "*Qui bona egerunt ibunt in uitam eternam: / Qui uero mala, in ignem eternum.*"[81] Thus the grim nature of the final passus reminds us that only a short time is left within the Christian era. Since mercy will soon be suspended, the Church must earnestly attempt to carry out *redde quod debes;* Conscience's vow of pilgrimage to find Piers may be a first step toward this. The effect of the message *redde quod debes* on the Dreamer is ambiguous, but it is interesting that he falls into this last sleep "In myddes of the masse tho men ʒeden to offrynge" (XXII. 4).[82] Although the visions of *Dobet* prompted him to go to mass, his somnolence has already allowed him to avoid making one gesture of *redde quod debes*. He does, however, wake at an opportune moment, as Conscience "gradde after grace" (XXIII. 386).

In summary, then, the Harrowing can be seen as the focal point around which the entire poem revolves. In terms of the historical allegory underlying the contemporary level of action, the *Visio* points to a time when confession can be answered by mercy rather than hope, when concern with physical sustenance is overshadowed by concern with spiritual,[83]

---

[79] The similarities between the *Visio* and *Dobest* have been made clear by Raw (146) and Carruthers (*Search* 153–156).

[80] I believe that Langland uses the term "Antichrist" in connection with the historical allegory of the poem, thus signaling the impending Judgment. However, Frank ("The Conclusion of *Piers Plowman,*" *Journal of English and Germanic Philology* 49 [1950]) notes that by the fourteenth century "Antichrist" was a mere term of abuse: "By Antichrist, therefore, Langland means either the Pope, as the one responsible for this league of ecclesiastics and sins, or else all Christians, but especially churchmen, who by their evil lives or corruptions of doctrine and sacraments lead men to sin rather than to grace" (314). The *Encyclopaedia of Religion and Ethics* (W. Bousset, "Antichrist," 1913 ed.) confirms that "Thus the time came when people saw Antichrist, or the forerunner of Antichrist, in every ecclesiastical, political, national, or social opponent, and the catch-word 'Antichrist' sounded on all sides."

[81] J.A. Burrow, *Ricardian Poetry* (New Haven: Yale University Press, 1971), notes that "there is no return to the Malvern Hills. Yet the end of his last dream does carry us back, most readers have felt, to the beginning of the poem. . . . This circularity creates an effect very different from the 'endless round' of *Pearl*. Endlessness in *Pearl* means eternity; in *Piers* it signifies the cycle of spiritual growth and decay which will go on until the end of time, both in individuals and in institutions" (66).

[82] His falling asleep at this point in the mass also explains the fact that the figure he sees resembles both Jesus and Piers (XXII. 4–11), for the Host is first seen in the mass immediately after the offering (Kirk 184).

[83] Of course, Passus XXII is not the first to include the use of allegorical food. In the banquet scene in Passus XVI, the loaf of contrition and Patience's bread of the Pater Noster are the first instances of this.

when the context of Piers' pardon is filled in to clarify its function as a true pardon. This fulfillment occurs in *Dobet*, with attention centered on the Harrowing because Jesus' mastery of Hell commences an era of mercy. Those who believed in His coming but were forced to await Him in Hell are the first beneficiaries of His charity. The new law for Christians becomes "dilige deum et proximum tuum." But Christ's speech in Hell, like the pardon from the Creed, reminds us that another Harrowing is foretold. Until that time, Christians must "redde quod debes," for they will receive justice, not mercy, at the Last Judgment.

The tension between justice and mercy (including such manifestations as truth and charity, law and love, works and grace) is a prominent feature of the poem. Piers' pardon, sent by Truth, is ineffective until Christ, or Charity, pays the ransom for man. In the same way, the text of the pardon is not a pardon until completed by Hope's letter calling for Charity—as the Old Testament is not complete without the New. (Remember Book's statement that he must be burned unless Christ conquers Hell, the act which reconciles Old Testament justice with New Testament mercy.[84]) The labor put into the half-acre yields no spiritual harvest until the Christian era of *Dobet* takes place. And neither pagan nor Christian can achieve salvation without cleaving to both law and love, as Trajan did, and as Christ indicated by claiming that He came to fulfill the law, not destroy it. Even Spes' letter is written on "a pece of an harde roche" (XX. 12), a reminder that love rests on law; i.e., the seal of the Cross will rest on a fragment of the Sinai tablet.

As we have seen, the Harrowing itself is the cosmic act which reconciles these opposites. Those who followed truth waited in Abraham's bosom for the arrival of charity, or Christ. And this act made possible the joining of works and grace, as Ymaginatif (once again, the figure that resolves the dialectic) teaches:

Ac grace is a gras ther-fore to don hem eft growe;
Ac grace groweth nat til goode wil gynne reyne,
And wokie thorwe good werkes wikkede hertes.
Ac er suche a wil wexe god hym-self worcheth,
And sent forth seint espirit to don loue sprynge;
Spiritus ubi uult spirat, et cetera.
So grace, with-oute grace of god and of good werkes,
May nat bee, bee thow siker thauh we bidde euer.   (XV. 23–29)

This is basically the Augustinian view: grace is needed to move man to good works, which in turn increase grace. And prevenient grace is freely accessible to all, according to Ymaginatif: "He [God] wol no wickede man be lost bote yf he wol hym-self" (XV. 135).

Thus throughout the poem, despite the Dreamer's attempts to evade responsibility for his soul, the message is clear that all men (even pagans)

---

[84] Vasta sees Book's purpose as verifying that the visions of *Dobet* come from God (131).

can achieve salvation—not through pardons, baptism, predestination, or learning, but through a blending of law and love, works and grace. It is appropriate, then, that when we see in *Dobest* a society corrupted by the *kynde* of human nature, the Dreamer cries for grace. Only grace can return this society to a remembrance of *redde quod debes*—performing charitable works which will stand them in good stead at the Judgment, when they must face the inexorable Old Testament justice of Piers' pardon.

VI. CONCLUSION

The fourteenth century in England was a watershed in theological history, with a decisive split occurring between philosophy and theology, reason and faith. Perhaps the most bitter controversy, however, emerged over the relative importance of grace and works in Christian salvation. Both sides carried their arguments to such an extreme that God seemed a practically incomprehensible Being. For this reason, the question of the virtuous pagan became an important concern for both theologians and laymen; if the criteria for pagan salvation could be determined, the divine scheme as a whole might well be illuminated.

Both the Bible and tradition taught that, because of the taint of Adam's sin, all men who lived before the Christian era were confined in Hell. By the accident of chronology, they were "pagans"—i.e., non-Christians—even if they had anticipated the coming of a Messiah. Thus Christ's actions when He descended to Hell, and the identification of the souls He harrowed, were significant concerns. From the standpoint of human reason, it seemed that the offer of salvation should be extended to all, regardless of chronology or geography—hence such theories as Christ's preaching in Hell, the efficacy of implicit faith, even Uthred of Boldon's *clara visio.*

Most important, however, was the simple act of the Harrowing. By offering Himself as a ransom for fallen man and establishing His sovereignty over Hell, Christ initiated a new era of mercy. Was it conceivable, then, that this mercy could be extended to deserving pagans who had not been liberated during the Harrowing? The popular imagination adduced an affirmative answer in the case of Trajan, and the idea of the virtuous pagan blossomed in legends and secular literature.

Surprisingly, however, the secular authors who are the focus of this study demonstrate a conservative approach compared to the century's theologians, on the whole achieving a balance between grace and works. The *Erkenwald*-poet makes clear the value of human merit in the miraculous preservation of the judge's body, but his physical glorification simultaneously illustrates the extent of natural virtue. The spiritual preservation which the judge hungers for comes only through grace, signified in the poem by the bishop's baptismal tears. On the other hand, the Dreamer in *Piers Plowman* seeks to assure himself of salvation by engaging in fruitless intellectual inquiry, relying on his Christian baptism to satisfy his shortcomings. Ymaginatif, aided by the figure of the unbaptized Trajan, informs him that good works are also necessary. Thus these two poems nicely balance each other on the issue of grace (or baptism) vs. works: neither alone will suffice for salvation.

Even more important than determining the theological orientation of the poems, however, is gleaning new insights about the literature itself by analyzing the use of the theme of the virtuous pagan and the related theme of the Harrowing. In *St. Erkenwald,* by realizing that the judge has been deliberately left behind during the Harrowing, we recognize Erkenwald as a Christ-surrogate. Erkenwald's own "harrowing" of this pagan soul celebrates the continuing power of Christ's mercy and His continuing reign over Hell. At the same time, Erkenwald's miracle serves as a reminder that it is the duty of the Church Militant to continue to "harrow Hell," albeit by the more conventional method of converting unbelievers to the true faith and thus depriving Satan of gaining power over their souls.

The Harrowing is an important concept in *Piers Plowman* as well, where it serves as the thematic climax of the poem read as an historical allegory. The *Visio, Dobet,* and *Dobest* characterize respectively the Old Covenant, the New Covenant, and the impending end of the New Covenant in Judgment. In the poem, as in divine history, all events either look forward to or look back upon the Harrowing, which introduced mercy into the scheme of divine justice. Whereas *St. Erkenwald* emphasizes the positive aspects of the Harrowing, however, *Piers Plowman* closes with emphasis on the negative. Although the Harrowing did initiate an era of mercy, that time is near an end, and the final Harrowing, or Doomsday, is imminent. Langland's clergy, unlike Erkenwald, are portrayed as unworthy successors of Christ, and the Church as a whole has neglected its duty to *redde quod debes.*

Ultimately, neither poem offers a definitive answer as to the requirements for salvation. Men are certainly accountable for their works—the judge's justness accords him special dispensation in *St. Erkenwald,* and each Christian must *redde quod debes* in *Piers Plowman.* Yet it is grace which allows the judge to partake of the heavenly banquet, and *Piers Plowman* closes with Conscience's cry after grace. In each instance, the workings of grace are indisputable and yet unknowable—the only answer the medieval Church could devise for the paradox of the virtuous pagan.

BIBLIOGRAPHY
Primary Sources

Abelard, Peter. *Dialogus inter philosophum, Judaeum et Christianum. P.L.*, Vol. 178, cols. 1611–1684.
——. *Epistola XVII. P.L.*, Vol. 178, cols. 375–378.
——. *Expositio in Epistola Pauli Ad Romanos, Liber II. P.L.*, Vol. 178, cols. 831–880.
——. *Introductio ad Theologia Christiana. P.L.*, Vol. 178, cols. 979–1114.
——. *Theologia Christiana, Liber II. P.L.*, Vol. 178, cols. 1165–1212.
Alain of Lille. *De Fide Catholica: Contra Haereticos, Valdenses, Iudaeos et Paganos. P.L.*, Vol. 210, cols. 305–430.
Anselm. *Cur Deus Homo, Liber I. P.L.*, Vol. 158, cols. 359–400.
——. *Liber Meditationum et Orationum, Meditatio XI. P.L.*, Vol. 158, Cols. 762–769.
——. *Monologium LXXVII. P.L.*, Vol. 158, col. 219.
——. *Proslogion. P.L.*, Vol. 158, cols. 223–292.
Aquinas, Thomas. *Opera Omnia.* Ed. Stanislau E. Fretté and Pauli Maré. Paris: Ludovicum Vivès, Bibliopolam Editorem, 1871–80.
——. *Summa Theologiae.* Blackfriars in conjunction with McGraw-Hill, New York, and Eyre and Spottiswoode, London, 1964–66.
Augustine. *De Doctrina Christiana. P.L.*, Vol. 34, cols. 15–122.
——. *De Praesentia Dei Liber, seu Epistola CLXXXVII. P.L.*, Vol. 33, cols. 832–848.
——. *Epistola CLXIV. P.L.*, Vol. 33, cols. 709–718.
——. *Epistola CXC. P.L.*, Vol. 33, cols. 857–866.
——. *Sermo de Symbolo. P.L.*, Vol. 40, cols. 1190–1202.
Bernard of Clairvaux. *Contra Quaedam Capitula Errorum Abelardi. P.L.*, Vol. 182, cols. 1053–1072.
——. *De Consideratione, Liber V. P.L.*, Vol. 182, cols. 787–808.
——. *Epistola CLXXVIII. P.L.*, Vol. 182, cols. 351–353.
——. *Epistola CXC. P.L.*, Vol. 182, cols. 1053–1072.
——. *Epistola seu Tractatus, De Baptismo. P.L.*, Vol. 182, cols. 1031–1046.
——. *Sermo IV, De Sinu Abrahae. P.L.*, Vol. 183, cols. 471–475.
——. *Sermones in Cantica, Sermo XXXVI. P.L.*, Vol. 183, cols. 967–971.
Biblia Sacra, Vulgatae Editionis. Italy: Marietti, 1965.
Biblia Sacra Vulgata. Ed. Robertus Weber. Stuttgart: Württembergische Bibelanstalt, 1969.
Dante Alighieri. *The Divine Comedy of Dante Alighieri.* Trans. with parallel text by John D. Sinclair. 1939. New York: Oxford University Press, 1981.
The Earliest Life of Gregory the Great. Ed. and trans. Bertram Colgrave. Lawrence, Kan.: University of Kansas Press, 1968.
Gregory. *Epistola XV. P.L.*, Vol. 77, cols. 869–870..
——. *XL Homilarium in Evangelia, Liber II, Homilia XXVI. P.L.*, Vol. 76, cols. 1197–1204.
——. *Homilarium in Ezechielem, Liber II, Homilia V. P.L.*, Vol. 76, cols. 984–998.
Hugh of St. Victor. *De Sacramentis, Liber I, Pars X. P.L.*, Vol. 176, cols. 327–344.
Langland, William. *The Vision of William Concerning Piers the Plowman by William Langland.* Ed. Walter W. Skeat. Oxford: Clarendon Press, 1886.
Lombard, Peter. *Sententiarum Libri Quatuor, Liber III, Distinctio XXV. P.L.*, Vol. 192, cols. 809–811.
Maurus, Rabanus. *Commentarium in Exodum, Liber IV. P.L.*, Vol. 108, cols. 189–246.
Origen: Contra Celsum. Tr. Henry Chadwick. Cambridge: Cambridge University Press, 1953.
Saint Erkenwald. Ed. Clifford Peterson. Philadelphia: University of Pennsylvania Press, 1977.
St. Patrick's Purgatory. EETS 87. Ed. Carl Horstmann. London: Trübner and Co., 1887.
Tertullian. *De Anima.* Ante-Nicene Christian Library, Vol. XV. Ed. Rev. Alexander Roberts and James Donaldson. Edinburgh: T. and T. Clark, 1870.
The Tripartite Life of St. Patrick, with Other Documents Relating to That Saint. Ed. and trans. Whitley Stokes. London, 1887.
Virgil. *The Aeneid of Virgil.* Trans. Rolfe Humphries. New York: Charles Scribner's Sons, 1951.
Voragine, Jacobus de. *Legenda Aurea.* Ed. Th. Graesse. Osnabrück: Otto Zeller, 1965.

Secondary Sources

Adams, John F. *"Piers Plowman* and the Three Ages of Man." *Journal of English and Germanic Philology* 61 (1962): 23–41.

Adams, Robert. "Piers's Pardon and Langland's Semi-Pelagianism." *Traditio* 39 (1983): 367–418.

Alford, John A. "Literature and Law in Medieval England." *PMLA* 92 (1977): 941–951.

Ames, Ruth A. *The Fulfillment of the Scriptures: Abraham, Moses, and Piers.* Evanston, Illinois: Northwestern University Press, 1970.

Baker, Denise N. "Dialectic Form in *Pearl* and *Piers Plowman.*" *Viator* 15 (1984): 263–273.

——. "From Plowing to Penitence: *Piers Plowman* and Fourteenth Century Theology." *Speculum* 55 (1980): 715–725.

Baldwin, Anna. "The Double Duel in *Piers Plowman* B. XVIII and C. XXI." *Medium Aevum* 50 (1981): 64–78.

Banner, William A. "Origen and the Tradition of Natural Law Concepts." *Dumbarton Oaks Papers* 8. Cambridge, Mass.: Harvard University Press, 1954. 51–82.

Barr, James. "Allegory and Typology." *A New Dictionary of Christian Theology.* Ed. Alan Richardson and John Bowden. 1983 ed.

Barth, Karl. *Anselm: Fides Quaerens Intellectum.* Trans. Ian W. Robertson. London: SCM Press Ltd., 1960.

Batard, Yvonne. *Dante, Minerve, et Apollon.* Paris: Société d'édition Les Belles Lettres, 1952.

Benson, C.D. "Augustinian Irony in *Piers Plowman.*" *Notes and Queries* 221 (1976): 51–54.

Benson, Larry D. "The Authorship of *St. Erkenwald.*" *Journal of English and Germanic Philology* 64 (1965): 393–405.

——. "The Pagan Coloring of *Beowulf.*" In *Old English Poetry: Fifteen Essays.* Ed. Robert P. Creed. Providence, R.I.: Brown University Press, 1967. 193–214.

Birnes, William J. "Christ as Advocate: The Legal Metaphor of *Piers Plowman.*" *Annuale Mediaevale* 16 (1975): 71–93.

Blackburn, F.A. "The Christian Coloring in *Beowulf.*" In *An Anthology of Beowulf Criticism.* Ed. Lewis E. Nicholson. Freeport, N.Y.: Books for Libraries Press, 1963. 1–22.

Bloomfield, Morton. "Patristics and Old English Literature: Notes on Some Poems." *Comparative Literature* 14 (1962): 36–43.

——. *Piers Plowman as a Fourteenth Century Apocalypse.* New Brunswick, N.J.: Rutgers University Press, 1962.

——. "Present State of *Piers Plowman* Studies." *Speculum* 14 (1939): 215–232.

Bousset, W. "Antichrist." *Encyclopaedia of Religion and Ethics.* Ed. James Hastings. 1913 ed.

Bowers, John M. *The Crisis of Will in Piers Plowman.* Washington, D.C.: Catholic University of America Press, 1986.

Boyde, Patrick. *Dante, Philomythes and Philosopher.* Cambridge: Cambridge University Press, 1981.

Brilioth, Yngve. *Eucharistic Faith and Practice Evangelical and Catholic.* Trans. A.G. Hebert. London: Society for Promoting Christian Knowledge, 1930.

Burn, A.E. "Creeds." In *Encyclopaedia of Religion and Ethics.* Ed. James Hastings. 1913 ed.

——. *An Introduction to the Creeds and to the Te Deum.* London: Methuen and Co., 1899.

Burrow, John. "The Action of Langland's Second Vision." In *Style and Symbolism in Piers Plowman.* Ed. Robert J. Blanch. Knoxville, Tenn.: University of Tennessee Press, 1969. 209–227.

——. 'The Audience of *Piers Plowman.*" *Anglia* 75 (1957): 373–384.

——. *Ricardian Poetry.* New Haven: Yale University Press, 1971.

Cairns, Sandra. "Fact and Fiction in the Middle English *De Erkenwaldo.*" *Neuphilologische Mitteilungen* 83 (1982): 430–438.

Calisch, Edward N. *The Jew in English Literature.* 1909. Port Washington, N.Y.: Kennikat Press, Inc., 1969.

Capéran, Louis. *Le problème du salut des infidèles, essai historique et essai théologique.* Toulouse: Grand Séminaire, 1934.

Carruthers, Mary. *The Search for St. Truth: A Study of Meaning in Piers Plowman.* Evanston, Ill.: Northwestern University Press, 1973.

——. "Time, Apocalypse, and the Plot of *Piers Plowman.*" In *Acts of Interpretation: The Text in Its Contexts, 700–1600: Essays on Medieval and Renaissance Literature in Honor of E. Talbot Donaldson.* Ed. Mary Carruthers and Elizabeth Kirk. Norman, Okla: Pilgrim, 1982. 175–188.

Chadwick, Henry. *Early Christian Thought and the Classical Tradition.* New York: Oxford University Press, 1966.

Chambers, R.W. "Long Will, Dante, and the Righteous Heathen." *Essays and Studies by Members of the English Association* 9 (1924): 50–69.

———. *Man's Unconquerable Mind.* London: Jonathan Cape, 1939.

Charity, A.C. *Events and Their Afterlife: The Dialectics of Christian Typology in the Bible and Dante.* Cambridge: Cambridge University Press, 1966.

Chroust, A.H. "Contribution to the Medieval Discussion: 'utrum Aristoteles sit salvatus.' " *Journal of the History of Ideas* 6 (1945): 231–238.

Clark, Susan L. and Julian N. Wasserman. "*St. Erkenwald's* Spiritual Itinerary." *American Benedictine Review* 33 (1982): 257–269.

Coghill, Nevill. "The Character of Piers Plowman Considered from the B Text." *Medium Aevum* 2 (1933): 108–135.

Coleman, Janet. *Medieval Readers and Writers 1350–1400.* New York: Columbia University Press, 1981.

———. *Piers Plowman and the Moderni.* Rome: Edizioni di storia e letteratura, 1981.

———. "*Sublimes et Litterati:* The Audience for the Themes of Grace, Justification and Predestination, Traced from the Disputes of the Fourteenth Century *Moderni* to the Vernacular *Piers Plowman.*" Ph.D. diss., Yale University 1970.

Daniélou, Jean. *Holy Pagans of the Old Testament.* Trans. Felix Faber. New York: Longmans, Green and Co., 1957.

———. *The Theology of Jewish Christianity.* Trans. and ed. John A. Baker. Chicago: H. Regnery Co., 1964.

Davidson, Arnold E. "Mystery, Miracle, and Meaning in *St. Erkenwald.*" *Papers on Language and Literature* 16 (1979): 37–44.

Davis, Charles T. *Dante and the Idea of Rome.* Oxford: Clarendon Press, 1957.

Davlin, Sister Mary C., O.P. "*Kynde Knowyng* as a Major Theme in *Piers Plowman B.*" *Review of English Studies,* n.s. 22 (1971): 1–19.

Day, Mabel. "'Mele Tyme of Seintes,' *Piers Plowman,* B, V, 500." *Modern Language Review* 27 (1932): 317–318.

Donahue, Charles. "*Beowulf* and Christian Tradition: A Reconsideration from a Celtic Stance." *Traditio* 21 (1965): 55–116.

———. "*Beowulf,* Ireland, and the Natural Good." *Traditio* 7 (1949–51): 263–278.

Donaldson, E.T. *Piers Plowman: The C-Text and Its Poet.* New Haven: Yale University Press, 1949.

Donna, Sister Rose Bernard. *Despair and Hope: A Study in Langland and Augustine.* Washington, D.C.: Catholic University of America Press, 1948.

Dugdale, Sir William. *History of St. Paul's Cathedral.* London: T. Warren, 1658.

Dunning, T.P. "Langland and the Salvation of the Heathen." *Medium Aevum* 12 (1943): 45–54.

Evans, G.R. *Alan of Lille, the Frontiers of Theology in the Later Twelfth Century.* Cambridge: Cambridge University Press, 1983.

Evans, W.O. "Charity." In *Piers Plowman: Critical Approaches.* Ed. S.S. Hussey. London: Methuen and Co., Ltd., 1969. 245–278.

Every, George. *Christian Mythology.* New York: Hamlyn, 1970.

Faigley, Lester L. "Typology and Justice in *St. Erkenwald.*" *American Benedictine Review* 29 (1978): 381–390.

Ferguson, J. *Pelagius: A Historical and Theological Study.* Cambridge: Cambridge University Press, 1956.

Foster, Kenelm. "Religion and Philosophy in Dante." In *The Mind of Dante.* Ed. U. Limentani. Cambridge: Cambridge University Press, 1965. 47–78.

———. *The Two Dantes and Other Studies.* London: Darton, Longman and Todd, 1977.

Frank, Robert Worth, Jr. "The Conclusion of *Piers Plowman.*" *Journal of English and Germanic Philology* 49 (1950): 309–316.

———. *Piers Plowman and the Scheme of Salvation: An Interpretation of Dowel, Dobet, and Dobest.* Yale Studies in English 136. New Haven: Yale University Press, 1957.

Frend, W.H.C. *Martyrdom and Persecution in the Early Church.* Garden City, N.Y.: Doubleday and Co., Inc., 1967.

Frezza, Mario. *Il problema della salvezza dei pagina (da Abelardo al Seicento).* Napoli: Fiorentino, 1962.

Gaffney, Wilbur. "The Allegory of the Christ-Knight in *Piers Plowman.*" *PMLA* 46 (1931): 155–168.

Gardner, Edmund G. *Dante's Ten Heavens: A Study of the Paradiso.* London: Archibald Constable and Co. Ltd., 1904.

Gilson, Étienne. *Reason and Revelation in the Middle Ages.* New York: Charles Scribner's Sons, 1954.

Goldsmith, Margaret E. "The Christian Perspective in *Beowulf.*" In *An Anthology of Beowulf Criticism.* Ed. Lewis E. Nicholson. Freeport, N.Y.: Books for Libraries Press, 1963. 373–386.

——. *The Figure of Piers Plowman: The Image on the Coin.* Piers Plowman Studies II. Cambridge: D.S. Brewer, 1981.

Gradon, Pamela. "*Trajanus redivivus:* Another Look at Trajan in *Piers Plowman.*" In *Middle English Studies Presented to Norman Davis in Honor of His Seventieth Birthday.* Ed. Douglas Gray and E.G. Stanley. Oxford: Clarendon Press, 1983. 93–114.

Grandgent, C.H., ed. *La Divina Commedia.* By Dante Alighieri. Rev. by Charles S. Singleton. Cambridge, Mass.: Harvard University Press, 1972.

Gumpel, Peter. "Unbaptized Infants: May They Be Saved?" *Downside Review* 72 (1964): 342–458.

Hahn, Thomas. "God's Friends: Virtuous Heathen in Later Medieval Thought and English Literature." Ph.D. diss., UCLA 1974.

——. "I 'gentili' e 'un uom nasce a la riva / de l'Indo.'" *L'Alighieri* 18.2 (1977): 3–8.

——. "The Indian Tradition in Western Intellectual History." *Viator* 9 (1978): 213–234.

Hamilton, Marie Padgett. "The Religious Principle in *Beowulf.*" In *An Anthology of Beowulf Criticism.* Ed. Lewis E. Nicholson. Freeport, N.Y.: Books for Libraries Press, 1963. 105–136.

Harent, S. "Infidèles—Salut des." *Dictionnaire de Théologie Catholique.* 3rd edition. 1923–1950.

Harwood, Britton J. "*Liberum Arbitrium* in the C-Text of *Piers Plowman.*" *Philological Quarterly* 52 (1973): 680–695.

Hibbard, Laura A. "Erkenbald the Belgian: A Study in Medieval Exempla of Justice." *Modern Philology* 17 (1920): 669–678.

Holleran, J.V. "The Role of the Dreamer in *Piers Plowman.*" *Annuale Mediaevale* 7 (1966): 33–50.

Hort, Greta. *Piers Plowman and Contemporary Religious Thought.* New York: Macmillan, 1937.

Hutchings, William. "'The Unintelligible Terms of an Incomprehensible Damnation': Samuel Beckett's *The Unnamable, Skeol,* and *St. Erkenwald.*" *Twentieth Century Literature* 27 (1981): 97–112.

James, M.R. *The Apocryphal New Testament.* 1924. Oxford: Oxford at the Clarendon Press, 1950.

Kane, George. *Middle English Literature: A Critical Study of the Romances, the Religious Lyrics, Piers Plowman.* London: Methuen and Co., Ltd., 1951.

——. *Piers Plowman: The Evidence for Authorship.* London: Athlone Press, 1965.

Kelly, J.N.D. *The Athanasian Creed.* London: Adam and Charles Black, 1964.

Kirk, Elizabeth D. *The Dream Thought of Piers Plowman.* New Haven: Yale University Press, 1972.

Kirk, Rudolf. "References to the Law in *Piers Plowman.*" *PMLA* 48 (1932): 322–327.

Knight, S.T. "Satire in *Piers Plowman.*" In *Piers Plowman: Critical Approaches.* Ed. S.S. Hussey. London: Methuen and Co., Ltd., 1969. 279–309.

Knowles, M.D. "The Censured Opinions of Uthred of Boldon." *Proceedings of the British Academy* 37 (1951): 305–342.

Lally, Tim D.P. "The Gothic Aesthetic of the Middle English *St. Erkenwald.*" *Ball State University Forum* 20/3 (1979): 2–10.

Lawlor, John. "The Imaginative Unity of *Piers Plowman.*" In *Style and Symbolism in Piers Plowman.* Ed. Robert J. Blanch. Knoxville, Tenn.: University of Tennessee Press, 1969. 101–116.

——. *Piers Plowman: An Essay in Criticism.* New York: Barnes and Noble, 1962.

——. "*Piers Plowman:* The Pardon Reconsidered." *Modern Language Review* 45 (1950): 449–458.

Lawton, D.A. "*Piers Plowman:* On Tearing—and Not Tearing—the Pardon." *Philological Quarterly* 60 (1981): 414–422.

Leff, Gordon. *Bradwardine and the Pelagians.* Cambridge: Cambridge University Press, 1957.

——. *Richard FitzRalph, Commentator of the Sentences.* Manchester: Manchester University Press, 1963.

Lönnroth, Lars. "Noble Heathen: A Theme in the Sagas." *Scandinavian Studies* 41 (1969): 1–29.

MacCulloch, J.A. *The Harrowing of Hell: A Comparative Study of an Early Christian Doctrine.* Edinburgh: T. and T. Clark, 1930.

McAlindon, T. "Hagiography into Art: A Study of *St. Erkenwald.*" *Studies in Philology* 67 (1970): 472–494.

McCully, John Raymond, Jr. "Conceptions of *Piers Plowman:* 1550 to 1970's." Ph.D. diss., Rice University 1976.

McLeod, Susan H. "The Tearing of the Pardon in *Piers Plowman.*" *Philological Quarterly* 56 (1977): 14–26.

McNamara, John F. "Responses to Ockhamist Theology in the Poetry of the *Pearl*-Poet, Langland, and Chaucer." Ph.D. diss., Louisiana State University 1968.

Maguire, Mother Catherine Elizabeth, R.S.C.J. "Franciscan Elements in the Thought of *Piers Plowman.*" Ph.D. diss., Fordham University 1950.

Marcett, M.E. *Uhtred of Boldon, Friar William Jordan and Piers Plowman.* New York: The Author, 1938.

Meroney, Howard. "The Life and Death of Longe Wille." *English Literary History* 17 (1950): 1–35.

Metlizski, Dorothee. *The Matter of Araby in Medieval England.* New Haven: Yale University Press, 1977.

Mills, David. "The Role of the Dreamer in *Piers Plowman.*" In *Piers Plowman: Critical Approaches.* Ed. S.S. Hussey. London: Methuen and Co., Ltd., 1969. 180–212.

Minnis, A.J. *Chaucer and Pagan Antiquity.* Totowa, N.J.: Rowman and Littlefield, 1982.

Modder, Montagu F. *The Jew in the Literature of England.* 1939. New York: Meridian Books, Inc., 1960.

Monnier, Jean. *La descente aux enfers: étude de pensée religieuse, d'art et de littérature.* Paris: Librairie Fischbacher, 1905.

Moorman, Charles. "Essential Paganism of Beowulf." *Modern Language Quarterly* 28 (1967): 3–18.

Morse, Ruth, ed. *St. Erkenwald.* Totowa, N.J.: Rowman and Littlefield, 1975.

Murtaugh, Daniel M. *Piers Plowman and the Image of God.* Gainesville: University of Florida Press, 1978.

Muscatine, Charles. *Poetry and Crisis in the Age of Chaucer.* Notre Dame: University of Notre Dame Press, 1972.

Obermann, Heiko. "Facientibus quod in se est Deus non denegat gratium: Robert Holcot OP and the Beginning of Luther's Theology." *Harvard Theological Review* 55 (1962): 317–342.

O'Driscoll, Philomena. "The Dowel Debate in *Piers Plowman B.*" *Medium Aevum* 50 (1981): 18–29.

Overstreet, Samuel A. "'Grammaticus Ludens': Theological Aspects of Langland's Grammatical Allegory." *Traditio* 40 (1984): 252–296.

Panitz, Esther L. *The Alien in Their Midst.* East Brunswick, N.J.: Associated University Presses, Inc., 1981.

Pantin, William. *The English Church in the Fourteenth Century.* Cambridge: Cambridge University Press, 1955.

Paris, Gaston. *La légende de Trajan.* Paris: Imprimerie Nationale, 1878.

Patrides, C.A. "Salvation of Satan." *Journal of the History of Ideas* 28 (1967): 467–478.

Patrologia Latina. Ed. Jacques Paul Migne. Paris: Garnier fratres et J.P. Migne successores, 1865–80.

Paull, Michael R. "Mahomet and the Conversion of the Heathen in *Piers Plowman.*" *English Language Notes* 10 (1972): 1–8.

Pearsall, Derek, ed. *Piers Plowman by William Langland: An Edition of the C-Text.* Berkeley and Los Angeles: University of California Press, 1979.

Peck, Russell. "Number Structure in *St. Erkenwald.*" *Annuale Mediaevale* 14 (1973): 9–21.

Pelikan, Jaroslav. *The Christian Tradition: A History of the Development of Doctrine.* Chicago: University of Chicago Press, 1978.

Pelzer, A. "Les 51 Articles de Guillaume Occam censurés en Avignon en 1326." *Revue d'histoire écclesiastique* 18 (1922): 240–271.

Petronella, Vincent F. "*St. Erkenwald:* Style as the Vehicle for Meaning." *Journal of English and Germanic Philology* 66 (1967): 532–540.

Pézard, A. "Riphée ou la naissance d'un mythe." *Revue des Études Italiennes* 25 (1979): 5–40.

Quasten, Johannes. *The Beginnings of Patristic Literature.* Vol. I of *Patrology.* Westminster, Md.: Newman Press, 1951.

Quilliet, H. "Descente de Jésus aux enfers." *Dictionnaire de Théologie Catholique.* 3rd ed. 1924.

Quirk, Randolph. "Langland's Use of Kynde Wit and Inwit." *Journal of English and Germanic Philology* 52 (1953): 182–188.

Raw, Barbara. "Piers and the Image of God in Man." In *Piers Plowman: Critical Approaches.* Ed. S.S. Hussey. London: Methuen and Co., Ltd., 1969. 142–179.

Reichardt, Paul F. "The Art and Meaning of the Middle English *St. Erkenwald.*" Ph.D. diss., Rice University 1971.

Renucci, Paul. *Dante, disciple et juge du monde Gréco-Latin.* Paris: Société d'édition Les Belles Lettres, 1954.

Rizzo, Gino. "Dante and the Virtuous Pagans." In *A Dante Symposium. In Commemoration of the 700th Anniversary of the Poet's Birth (1265–1965).* Ed. William DeSua and Gino Rizzo. University of North Carolina Studies in the Romance Languages and Literatures 58. Chapel Hill, N.C.: University of North Carolina Press, 1965. 115–140.

Robertson, D.W., Jr., and Bernard F. Huppé. *Piers Plowman and Scriptural Tradition.* Princeton: Princeton University Press, 1951.

Robson, J.A. *Wyclif and the Oxford Schools.* Cambridge: Cambridge University Press, 1961.

Ruffini, F. "Dante e il problema della salvezza degl'infideli." *Studi danteschi* 14 (1930): 79–92.

Russell, G.H. "The Salvation of the Heathen: The Exploration of a Theme in *Piers Plowman.*" *Journal of the Warburg and Courtauld Institute* 29 (1966): 101–116.

Savage, Henry L., ed. *St. Erkenwald: A Middle English Poem.* New Haven: Yale University Press, 1926.

Schroeder, Mary C(arruthers). "*Piers Plowman:* The Tearing of the Pardon." *Philological Quarterly* 49 (1970): 8–18.

Seeberg, Reinhold. *Text-Book of the History of Doctrines.* Trans. Charles E. Hay. Grand Rapids, Mich.: Baker Book House, 1952.

Sikes. J.G. *Peter Abailard.* Cambridge: Cambridge University Press, 1932.

Singleton, Charles. *Journey to Beatrice.* Vol. II of *Dante Studies.* Cambridge, Mass.: Harvard University Press, 1954.

Smith, Ben H. *Traditional Imagery of Charity in Piers Plowman.* Hague: Mouton, 1966.

Smith, Constance I. "Reply to '*Descendit ad inferos:* Medieval Views on Christ's Descent into Hell and the Salvation of the Ancient Just.'" *Journal of the History of Ideas* 30 (1969): 249–250.

Southern, R.W. *Western Views of Islam in the Middle Ages.* Cambridge, Mass.: Harvard University Press, 1962.

Stouck, Mary-Ann. "'Mournynge and Myrthe' in the Alliterative *St. Erkenwald.*" *Chaucer Review* 10 (1976): 243–254.

Sullivan, Sister Carmeline. *The Latin Insertions and the Macaronic Verse in Piers Plowman.* Washington, D.C.: Catholic University of America Press, 1932.

Tch'ang-Tche, J. Wang. *Saint Augustin et les vertus des paiens.* Paris: Gabriel Beauchesne et ses fils, 1938.

Thomas, M.E. *Medieval Skepticism and Chaucer.* New York: William-Frederick Press, 1950.

Thompson, Craig R., ed. *Erasmus: Inquisitio de Fide.* 2nd ed. 1950. Hamden, Conn.: Archon Books, 1975.

Thompson, David. "Dante's Virtuous Romans." *Dante Studies, with the Annual Report of the Dante Society* 96 (1978): 145–162.

Traver, Hope. *The Four Daughters of God.* Bryn Mawr College Monographs, Monograph Series 6. Philadelphia, Pa., 1907.

Trower, Katherine B. "The Figure of Hunger in *Piers Plowman.*" *American Benedictine Review* 24 (1973): 238–260.

———. "Temporal Tensions in the *Visio* of *Piers Plowman.*" *Mediaeval Studies* 35 (1973): 389–412.

Turner, R.V. "*Descendit ad inferos:* Medieval Views on Christ's Descent into Hell and the Salvation of the Ancient Just." *Journal of the History of Ideas* 27 (1966): 173–194.

Vasta, Edward. *The Spiritual Basis of Piers Plowman.* Studies in English 18. New York: Humanities Press, 1965.

Vickers, Nancy J. "Seeing Is Believing: Gregory, Trajan, and Dante's Art." *Dante Studies* 101 (1983): 67–85.

Vignaux, Paul. *Justification et prédestination au XIVᵉ siècle.* Paris: E. Leroux, 1934.

Wells, Henry W. "The Construction of *Piers Plowman.*" *PMLA* 44 (1929): 123–140.

———. "The Philosophy of *Piers Plowman.*" *PMLA* 53 (1938): 339–349.

Wenzel, Siegfried. "St. Erkenwald and the Uncorrupted Body." *Notes and Queries* 226 (1981): 13–14.

Wesling, Donald. "Eschatology and the Language of Satire in *Piers Plowman.*" *Criticism* 10 (1968): 277–289.

Whatley, Gordon. "Heathens and Saints: *St. Erkenwald* in Its Legendary Context." *Speculum* 61 (1986): 330–363.

———. "The Middle English *St. Erkenwald* and Its Liturgical Context." *Mediaevalia* 8 (1982): 277–306.

———. "The Uses of Hagiography: The Legend of Pope Gregory and the Emperor Trajan in the Middle Ages." *Viator* 15 (1984): 25–63.

———. "*Vita Erkenwaldi:* An Anglo-Norman's Life of an Anglo-Saxon Saint." *Manuscripta* 27 (1983): 67–81.

Wintersdorf, K.P. "*Beowulf:* The Paganism of Hrothgar's Danes." *Studies in Philology* 78 (1981): 91–119.

Wittig, Joseph S. "'Piers Plowman' Passus IX–XII: Elements in the Design of the Inward Journey." *Traditio* 28 (1972): 211–280.

Wolfson, H.A. *Philosophy of the Church Fathers.* Cambridge, Mass.: Harvard University Press, 1970.

Woolf, Rosemary. "The Tearing of the Pardon." In *Piers Plowman: Critical Approaches.* Ed. S.S. Hussey. London: Methuen and Co., 1969. 50–75.

Young, Karl. *The Harrowing of Hell in Liturgical Drama.* Transactions of the Wisconsin Academy of Sciences, Arts, and Letters. Vol. XVI, Part II. No. 2. 889–947.

INDEX

Abelard 18, 22, 26, 34
  view of Descent 17, 25
  view of pagan salvation 25
  view of reason 23-24
Abraham 10, 21
  in *Piers Plowman* 71, 80, 81. *See also* Faith
Abraham's bosom 13, 18-19, 21, 27
  in *St. Erkenwald* 55
  in *Piers Plowman* 79, 80, 81, 87
Adam 5, 8, 57, 69, 79, 89
  salvation of 7, 13, 14, 24, 34
Adam of Woodham 29, 31, 32
Alain of Lille 17, 20-22
Albigensians 20, 21, 22
Alexander B 4, 33, 34n
Alexander of Hales 17, 28
Ambrose 17n, 24, 36
Anselm 17n, 29
Antichrist 85, 86
apocatastasis 11
Apocryphon of Jeremiah 6
Aquinas 17, 21n, 22, 23, 29, 34, 64n
  tale of St. Macharius 37
  Trajan legend 42
  value of reason 25-26
  view of baptism 48, 65
  view of Descent 27
  view of Limbo 1, 43
  view of pagan salvation 1, 53
Aristotle 11, 28, 68, 69
Athanasian Creed 70, 76, 78
Augustine 24, 27, 29, 34, 55, 87
  irony, as used in *Piers Plowman* 68n
  view of baptism 36n, 48
  view of Descent 1, 13-16, 17
  view of Hell 12, 13
  view of pagan salvation 14, 44
  view of Rome 39n

baptism 2, 7, 8, 27, 32n
  in Dante 47-48
  in *Piers Plowman* 64-66
  in *St. Erkenwald* 55, 57, 58, 59
  legends of 36-37
  necessity of 1, 15
Beowulf 38
Bernard of Clairvaux 17, 18-19, 22
Book (character in *Piers Plowman*) 82, 87
Bradwardine, Thomas 30, 32, 38, 56, 57, 58n, 63
Brahman 33, 45n
Buckingham, Thomas 29, 31, 32

Cato 44-45, 48
Charity (character in *Piers Plowman*) 77
Charity, Tree of. *See* Tree of Charity
Chaucer, Geoffrey 3, 4, 33
Chrysostom, John 16
Clement of Alexandria 6, 9, 10, 11, 12, 16

Clergy (character in *Piers Plowman*) 66
Conscience (character in *Piers Plowman*) 77, 85, 86
Constantine 47
Cornelius 19-20, 26
Cyprian 1n, 48n

Damascene, John 37
Dante 1, 36, 49n
  Gregory/Trajan legend 4, 46-47
  treatment of virtuous pagans 3n, 43-48
  view of Rome 39
Descent of Christ 5-6, 34
  in Creed 26, 82
  purpose of 1, 6, 7, 9n, 10, 11, 12
  relationship to *St. Erkenwald* 52-53
  theological views of 10, 11, 12, 13-16, 17, 21, 22, 25, 27
  See also Harrowing
Devil 6, 79, 82. *See also* Lucifer, Satan
  deceit of 7, 17n
Diaconus, Johannes 40n, 42
Diaconus, Paulus 40n
Dinocrates 36
Donatist heresy 55

Elijah 8
Enenkel 41
Enoch 8, 21, 22
Epistle of the Apostles 7
Erasmus 1n
Erkenbald 51n
Evodius, Bishop 13, 16

Faith (character in *Piers Plowman*) 80, 81, 82, 83
faith
  explicit 26, 46-47, 48
  implicit 26, 34, 89
  double faith theory 9, 11
  single faith theory 12
Falconille 37
FitzRalph, Richard 30
Four Daughters of God 82, 83, 84

gnosticism 12n
Gospel of Nicodemus 6-8, 54, 82
Grace (character in *Piers Plowman*) 77
grace 2, 29n, 30, 31, 32, 89, 90
  in *Piers Plowman* 62-63, 69-70, 71, 74n, 75n, 77n, 87- 88
  in *St. Erkenwald* 57-58
  in Trajan legend 42
Gregory of Rimini 30
Gregory the Great 16, 23, 26
Gregory/Trajan legend 4, 42-43
  in Dante's *Divine Comedy* 46-47
  in *Piers Plowman* 64-65, 71
  in *St. Erkenwald* 50n-51n, 56

98